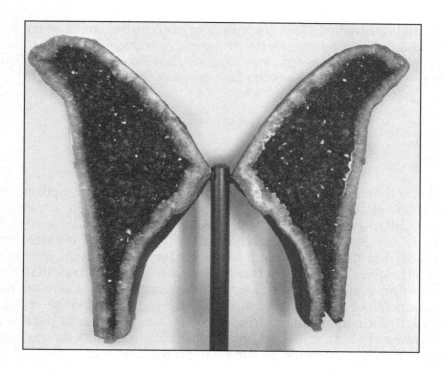

ISBN : 9781092662314
Debbie Hardy © 2019
Cover Image by Elisa Lee

Disclaimer

The author is not a medical practitioner, cannot give medical or psychological advice or diagnose patients, and cannot prescribe medications. Please consult your licensed medical practitioner if you have any health or psychological concerns. The information provided in this book is not a substitute for medical, legal, or other expert advice. Please be advised there are no guarantees that the following content will heal your specific situation, and there are no guarantees of specific results from following the guidance of this book. Information provided in this book is as accurate as possible; however, the author accepts no responsibility or liability for any loss or damage caused by the information given in this book.

Also by Debbie Hardy

Meditation Made Easy Using Crystals

If you have struggled with meditation or had difficulty clearing the chatter in your head, this is a must-read book for you! It also explains how to work on self-healing, connection to angels, and deeper soul connection by using crystals during meditation. It is geared toward all levels of meditation experience. The book provides a healing layout that you can do on your own, as well as a guided meditation—plus so much more! Available on Amazon.

"I would highly recommend this beautiful book to those just beginning with crystals, to those who want to review, or [those who want to] get a different point of view [on using] crystals in practical meditation or in general life use. Debbie speaks with a clarity of voice that is easy to resonate with. I could easily follow along with her writing style, and nothing felt jarring to me as I read. I found practical advice I'd like to incorporate into my daily wellness practice, as well as new information about high-vibration crystals that I'd love to explore. Very well done!" ~ Nightingeal

"I absolutely loved Debbie's book. It was easy to follow, and it even had a diagram of how [to] line your crystals to rid yourself of negative energy. The feeling was so wonderful. Afterward I followed the instructions to bring in the positive energy. It was awesome! I highly recommend it." ~ Mina

"I thoroughly enjoyed reading this book, because I have tried meditation in the past and was unable to meditate on my own. There was too much 'chatter' in my head, or I was influenced by outside distractions, or I couldn't set the proper mood...the list of excuses is endless. So I tried books. This list is also endless. Other books made meditation seem mysterious and complicated—to me, anyway. But here the author has demystified the practice of meditation, made it uncomplicated, and enhanced it with the use of crystals! I am still a beginner and may never reach the author's level of expertise, but one thing is for sure: this is not a book I will put down or put away. In fact, I have already started reading it for the second time! I have now been able to relax, de-stress, unwind, and not take everything so seriously Plus, I have started my own collection of crystals. Thank you, Debbie Hardy, for all you've taught me!" ~ Carol

Debbie Hardy

Spirit of the Crystal Ray:

Twenty-One Days of Channeled Guidance to Help You with Your Spiritual Journey

Love & Light

[signature]

Contents

I dedicate this book to all of those on their spiritual path.

When you follow your purpose, miracles happen.

Introduction

I have thought about writing a book about my experiences of channeled information while using high-vibration crystals in the past, but I put it off many times. It was actually something that was supposed to be a good portion of my first book, but that took a bit of a different direction once I really started writing it. My spiritual guidance led me to the concept and creation of this book. When I am given inspiration from my spirit guides, I find it best to follow that inspiration because I believe it will help me help others in some way, and I find a deep connection with my higher self at the same time.

I was given the process and structure of writing this book from my spirit guides, and I felt good about it, but I had one requirement of my own. I wanted this book to touch the reader at a deep level of their being as they read it. I wanted readers to feel a deep beauty within the words and to find a correlation between the messages and the challenges within their own lives. My spirit guides agreed with me. So as you read the following pages, I hope that you find something beautiful and something that touches you on a deeper level in some way. I am grateful that I listened to my spirit guides for the creation of this book, because I feel it has helped me within my own lessons. I also hope it will reach those who need it for their own path as well. We are not here to convince you or try to make you believe something; we are here to challenge you to think of things a little differently in order to help you on your path in some way.

Several years ago, when I was really focusing on my own self-healing, I went to a hypnotherapist often. Hypnosis or hypnotherapy is a way to use guided relaxation techniques and prompts to achieve a heightened state of awareness. It is very similar to deep meditation but with the use of a person guiding you through prompts. During those sessions, I learned a great deal of what I was capable of, and one of those things was channeling spirit. The practice of channeling involves entering a deep meditative state in order to receive guidance from spirit. I did not use crystals during those sessions, but I was guided and led on journeys (similar to guided meditations), and one day a spirit came through, and I began channeling while I was in the hypnotic state. The spirit was speaking through me and using my body and voice as a channel to convey its message. That happened rather unexpectedly, and I was surprised at the same time. After the first time, I was able to go under hypnosis and channel the same spirits each time.

During that time in my life, I was also very experienced at meditation and using crystals. So I decided to work with very high vibration crystals to go into a deep state of meditation similar to that of hypnosis. I attempted to channel spirit on my own without the guidance of a hypnotist, and with the crystals I was able to do so. High-vibration crystals maintain a higher frequency, which enables one to access higher realms, spiritual guidance, and ancient records during the state of meditation. I set a recording device by my side and took myself into deep meditation while holding a crystal such as apophyllite, danburite, cathedral lightbrary, elestial or devic temple, or other similar crystals, and I connected with the same spirit guides that I had been able to channel under the guidance of hypnosis. I recorded my personal channeled sessions so I would be able to listen them afterward. The more and more I practiced this, the easier it became to connect to spirit and channel their messages. Also, since I have had a deep connection to crystal energy for several years, I have found it easy to extract information stored within crystal energy. I use crystals as a portal for stored guidance and access to spirit guides. I can tap into other realms, many levels of spirit guides, and ancient wisdom by using crystals during meditation. Once you learn to do something it becomes easier and second nature. Plus you gain the confidence that you can repeat what you have learned with ease. So connecting to spirit and channeling just began to occur naturally and easily for me. As I mentioned, I was led by my spirit guides to share channeled information from the spirit realm, and when I purchased massive amethyst geode wings at a gem show, it became very clear to me that these wings would be the crystal energy source to help me channel the information I was to share with all who need it at this time.

It was during February 2018, at the Tucson Gem and Mineral Show in Arizona, that I came across these massive amethyst geode wings. My husband and I were shopping for crystals for my store, and we came across these grand amethyst geodes shaped like angel (or butterfly) wings. I had no intention of purchasing something so large at the time, but I walked by them and felt their energy. I got my picture taken as I stood in front of them, and it appeared as if the wings were sitting upon my back. I felt something about them that I had not felt with any other comparably sized geodes from the vendor. These wings had such a deep purple jelly color and large points that they really stood out to me. They weigh 265 kilograms (584 pounds), and they measure fifty-two inches across and sixty-four inches tall. Standing there next to them, I felt that the wings belonged upon me. They had been mined from the Brazilian region of Rio Grande do Sul. I was not considering purchasing something so grand, but I asked the price, and I was uncertain about spending that much money. The vendor said someone else was considering purchasing the geode, but I decided if it was meant to be, it would be. So we went on our way and continued shopping. I kept thinking about the wings; as a matter of fact, I could not get them out of my mind. So we decided if they were still there a bit later, maybe they were meant for me. As we walked around to the other vendors, I made a few calls to my bank for account information to be sure I had enough credit to manage such a purchase, and it came back rather quickly that I did. Imagine that. We finished our shopping and decided to go back and talk to the vendor once again. The wings were still available, so we agreed upon a final price, and I handed over the credit card. As I was signing the bill of sale, the other person who had inquired about them returned to purchase them, so it felt like they were truly meant to go home with me. It was all so surreal, and I still shake my head over the experience.

When I purchased the wings, I felt that I would be reselling them sometime, because I honestly felt that they belonged to someone else. However, I felt I would be their keeper for a period of time, and during that time I would work with them to see what story they had to tell. The pages that follow are just a drop in the bucket of the information they hold within them and what they have to share.

I had to wait two months for the geode to arrive, and just getting them off the truck and into my home was a huge undertaking. Four deliverymen took great care manoeuvring the massive wings inch by inch as they unloaded them and brought them to their current sitting space. My home is not big, and the wings take up a grand amount of space in my living room. I kept saying, "I cannot believe this. I cannot believe these are mine." Their energy is simply amazing. I noticed right away that they definitely had a masculine feel to them. They are very powerful and confident in their abilities. They were quite dusty from sitting in Arizona for several weeks, so I had to do some extensive cleaning on them. That in itself took several days. When I had finished, they shined brighter than I ever remember seeing them!

The angel wings were so massive that I had no doubt that each point held vast information. I was confident that I could use them to channel information and/or use them in meditation to extract information needed for guidance for myself and possibly others. I began meditation with them, and I received guidance that they had information to share. I was told to meditate with them for twenty-one days and record the information that came through. Then I had one of those aha moments that said I needed to record what was extracted and guided and to put it into a book. This is that book. The twenty-one days of extraction are not consecutive, and as you will see, each day has specific information just for that day, although you will see an overall connection or theme throughout.

A Note on Format

This book is broken down into sections: the actual channeled message conveyed for that day, my personal reflection on either what I learned from the day's message or what other information came to me from the experience, action steps for the reader to do, and a journaling section for the reader to write their own thoughts and insights they may receive.

The actual channeled messages were recorded using a voice-to-text format during each session. I allowed the spirits to use me as a channel to convey the messages that we need to hear or learn from. I turned on my recording device, and as I entered the deep state of meditation, I allowed the spirits to talk through me. After each session, I transferred the messages to my document, editing certain words that might not have come through correctly from the voice-to-text format and adding punctuation.

When the word "you" is used within the channeled text, it addresses all those who are reading the text as a collective whole, but keep in mind it might not be specific to your situation. You may resonate with certain sections while other days you might not. It will be a different experience for everyone. When you see the word "we" within the channeled text, that refers to either the spirit guides speaking the messages from the channeled sessions or to all spirit guides collectively. The channeled text is italicized, and quotation marks indicate that I am speaking or responding to the channeled information during the channeled sessions. Occasionally there is some text in parentheses; this is something that came to me for areas of clarification or further explanation when I was going through the editing process. Those are my thoughts, not the channeled spirits'. These messages start off rather straightforward and get deeper from there. Each day is rather different; some days are very deep, and other days are a bit lighter. I hope that you find yourself thinking about the messages and how they can relate to your life journey at this point in time.

The reflection section contains my personal reflection after each session. This can be what I believe the spirits are trying to tell us in a more fluid way, or it can be where I am still downloading guidance from the session, and that information needs to be conveyed as well. Quite often I will get "downloaded" information in between or after sessions, when the spirit gives me more insight or guidance to share.

The action section is a time for you to sit quietly and think about what comes to you after you read the day's message. There may be prompts to think about or questions for you to answer. Some days there are actual suggestions of things to try that correspond with the day's message. Some days may be more meaningful for you than others. You may have more insight or aha moments than other days. We are all learning, and though we are going on this journey together, we will all respond in different ways.

There is a journaling section after each chapter for you to write your thoughts and feelings about the daily messages. You can also record the insights and answers from the daily action prompts in this section. These insights may come through to you after you read sections and come up with your own conclusions of how the daily messages may or may not fit into your life at this point in time.

I have also included other information in between certain days that will discuss how I care for the wings, how I meditate with them, or anything else I feel may be of some interest or importance.

Final Thoughts Before We Get Started

This project has turned into a true documentation of the experience of meditation with these wings and the direct information I have received by doing so. As you read the following channeled messages, we (the spirit guides and I) ask that you keep an open mind. Each person that reads this will gravitate and relate to different sections than someone else. Perhaps you were led to read this book to help you on your own personal journey in some way. Think about what you read within these pages, and take time to reflect upon the words and what connections or conclusions you make for yourself from reading them. Perhaps you will find insight, awareness, inspiration, or even hidden emotions that need to surface to move you forward in your own personal spiritual journey and facilitate your own inner exploration of who you are deep within.

I appreciate your letting me be your guide as we explore what the spirit guides feel is important for us to know at this point in our lives. Are you ready to step into the purple ray of the amethyst geode wings?

Day 1

I sat comfortably in my reclining chair, and I placed my hand upon the purple points of the amethyst wings. I immediately felt a very strong and powerful yet sensitive and understanding energy within them. It was as if the power and confidence of masculine energy and the understanding and nurturing of feminine energy were combined as one.

I had barely touched the geode in meditation, and I felt a beautiful energy going from my hand up my arm and through my being. We exchanged energy; we became one and the same and I let myself drift into deep meditation. I entered the purple-ray cave. As I went inside, I was given the wisdom of what it shared with us. I was told I must devote time to working with these wings and share the information that comes through. Others would connect with, listen to, and understand what was provided from these meditations. It was part of my journey to share with the world what I learned from these types of meditations. I must continue to learn in order to teach. I would carry the gift of the purple ray forever. This was an opportunity to help many achieve their own self-healing and self-realization.

We want to start off these discussions talking about abundance. It seems as though most of the human mindset is focused on obtaining abundance and there is an overall sense of lack within their lives. Everyone can obtain abundance, but many are too focused on sadness or other negative emotions. They do not see. Their eyes are not open; their heart is not open. Abundance is already within you, each of you. You hold it; it is within the depths of your being. You may not see it or feel it, but it is there. You are already abundant, but it can feel like you are not until you start to see what is in front of you. See what you have. See who you are. See what you have obtained in terms of material things and knowledge within your life time. You have closed your eyes because you focus your attention on trying to gain things when in fact you have so much already. Your heart is not open because you have closed it off from truly feeling and being true to yourself. So many have denied their true feelings and in essence denied being themselves. Because you have closed your eyes and heart you do not see what you truly have within your physical world but also within your soul. Once you allow yourself to see and open your heart you will begin to notice all the beauty that you are part of and all of the abundance that is yours. It will also allow the flow of more wonderful things and occurrences to come to you.

We (spirit) do not feel emotion as humans do; however, we are concerned by this behavior and lack of understanding. Within the next days, we will convey what we feel is important for you to focus on in order to help your life path. This is the beginning of many lessons that we will share with you. The first step of this experience is to open your eyes and open your heart. This will assist you with the learning journey you are on, as well as, allowing yourself to truly see and feel. Be open to where this takes you.

I stepped out of the meditation and came back to reality, thanking spirits for the beginning of this journey and the information they had provided thus far. Once I stepped out of the wings, I felt very dizzy, and I felt the need to ground myself because it was such a powerful energy.

Grounding is the process of connecting to earth or using a grounding crystal to become stable and balanced again. Light headedness or dizziness may occur after deep meditative or channeling sessions so grounding can alleviate those symptoms.

Reflection on Day 1

I felt the beginning few days of meditation with the angel wings were a getting-to-know-you kind of phase. The first channeled message was very brief, yet the words were very powerful indeed. I needed to get a feel for their energy, and at the same time I needed to let my physical body adjust to the powerful energy that was channeled through me. The message I channeled on the first day was simple and straightforward. The guidance I was given after that message showed me that there would be many more deep discussions to follow, and that I needed to be consistent with my learning so I could be consistent with the teaching. I had no doubt there was a great deal to learn from these wings, and I thought the more I connected with them, the more I would be able to extract from them.

I am actually not surprised that the very first day was a brief talk about abundance. We as a culture are so fixated on abundance, but what abundance is, is different for each and every one of us. Oftentimes we find ourselves wanting something and feeling a lack of abundance because the feeling of want creates the feeling of lack. Abundance means very simply a large quantity of something. We all have abundance, yet we do not realize how much we really have within our own lives. Abundance comes in many forms—the relationships with loved ones and friends, material objects, knowledge, or something else. It really comes down to how you see and feel it, and if we open our eyes and hearts, then we become aware of how much abundance we really have. Once we have that realization, the flow of even more opens up to us in unimaginable ways.

Today's message that everyone can obtain abundance is something that I have believed for some time. I believe that each person on this earth can obtain abundance, but we are so caught up in our physical lives that we have forgotten our roots, what we are capable of, and that we are all deserving. We have closed our eyes to what is possible to obtain or achieve. We have blocked our hearts from feeling because we have been hurt in the past. Those hurts often prompt us to put up permanent walls around us, which block us from feeling and experiencing the good things that are right in front of us. We need to readjust our way of thinking and our belief in what we are capable of to open the doors to abundance. Our humanness wants to protect us from any harm, but sometimes in doing so, it also blocks us from really seeing what is right in front of our very own eyes.

Action for Day 1

Reflect on abundance for a moment.
Do you feel you are abundant?
Do you feel it is the human right to be abundant?
Do you feel there is enough for everyone?

Do you feel you are capable of achieving or obtaining what you want during this lifetime?

What other thoughts come to mind?

How do you feel about the statement "Open your eyes and open your heart"?

Journal whatever comes to mind when you answer these questions and when you reflect on the day's channeled message.

Journal for Day 1

_____

_____

_____

_____

_____

_____

_____

_____

_____

_____

_____

_____

_____

_____

_____

_____

_____

_____

_____

_____

_____

_____

_____

_____

_____

Day 2

Every time I go into meditation and a spirit comes through, I typically ask who they are or what their name is. I like to know if I am dealing with angels, gods, goddesses, or something else. So it is no surprise that on day two I went into the meditation with these wings and decided to ask who was speaking to me.

The very first thing I did as I entered the purple-ray geode of these wings was to ask, "What is your name? Who is speaking to me?" Then the names Andromadus and Andromeda came to me. I was thinking that it was only one spirit speaking to me, but I received two names. After more thought I realized it was one spirit that had an equal balance of masculine and feminine energy and that each energy went by a different name, even though it was one and the same spirit. Looking back at yesterday's session, it makes sense to me that there was a combination of masculine and feminine energy. Overall it was a grand combination of energy that provided this insight to us.

I stepped into the purple cave once again; I always saw myself wearing white when I did so. White is a symbol of purity, goodness, and innocence. I felt I came to this sacred space wearing white as a sign of respect but also with the understanding that this was a safe place to receive what was meant for us.

The world has been in turmoil for centuries; it will be for a while yet more. There will be a time of harmony once again in the future. When more and more awaken and follow the path of light, the shift will occur. It is not the time yet, so many still need to learn the lessons they set forth. Many in this time are not learning the lessons they set out to do. They will come back and try again, and each time they will get closer, so eventually it will reach the collective energy of harmony. ("Come back and try again" refers to reincarnation in the next life, the opportunity to learn the lessons that may have not been learned during this lifetime.) *Those of you who are on the enlightened path right now, and those of you who are learning and growing spiritually, will be the leaders of the harmony movement. The harmony movement is the action of focusing your attention on bringing harmony to earth once again. The more that do this, the sooner earth will return to a state of peace.*

In the following pages you will learn in more detail what can you can do to contribute to this effort. The more you learn who you are deep within the more you will realize what is important to focus your attention and energy on for the rest of your time here on earth. You will begin to see things differently, and you will begin to avoid trivial occurrences or untruthful situations because you will have an understanding they are not part of your path. You will begin to make wise decisions regarding your human life. Eventually, you will pass and return (reincarnate) *more enlightened than you are now. Everything you learn during this human life cycle will give you more understanding in the next life cycle. You will not have to go through certain learning phases again. Eventually because of the extensive knowledge you have gained throughout all of these human life experiences, you will be teaching and helping others to find their way.*

As I exited the cave, I bowed my head and placed my hands in prayer position, walked backward, and gave thanks for the information provided. The last thoughts the spirits shared with me as I exited the cave were:

Come back, and come back often. We have much work to do.

Reflection on Day 2

Day two provided a bit more information than day one, though I did not necessarily see a direct connection between the two messages. However I did feel that there was an overall message that would eventually present itself if we looked at all the messages as a whole.

This was the first time in my many meditations with spirit guides that I was given two names for one spirit guide. I believe the reason for that is so that we can learn from both types of energies at the same time.

I have never heard of "the Harmony Movement," but just saying those words brings such great energy to me. In the beginning there was harmony; I have seen it many times in my own meditations. Greed, jealousy, fear, and the human ego led to the corruption that humans have faced for thousands of years. The Harmony Movement is the enlightened path to achieve unity and peace here on earth once again.

Enlightenment means to be in the state of having a well-informed outlook and to be well educated or knowledgeable about a specific matter. When we reach enlightenment about where we came from, why we are here, what we set out to do here, and where we need to go, then we have a clear understanding of what is important in this lifetime. Those who are on the path of enlightenment can contribute to the Harmony Movement with their actions of mindfulness, peace, kindness, and unconditional love for all creation. When everyone has achieved that status, the world and all its inhabitants will return to a place of harmony. I do not know about you, but I am honored to be part of such a movement.

Action for Day 2

Take some quiet time to reflect upon today's message and answer these questions:
Do you feel you have experienced many lifetimes?
Do you feel like you are on a path of enlightenment?
Looking back at your life experiences, do you understand why things happened the way they did?
What are your thoughts about the Harmony Movement?
Do you feel that there was a time of harmony in the past and that it is possible to return to that in the future?
How does it make you feel to know that you will be a leader in the future to help others along the way?
Journal your answers and any thoughts that come to you.

Journal for Day 2

Day 3

There is so much information contained within the points of these wings, and each point holds specific information. Although I have not seen it happen, I feel that these amethyst points continue to grow, change, and expand just as we do.

As soon as I tapped into the meditation state with the wings, I was taken immediately into the amethyst cave of the purple ray. During this session I saw myself from above, looking down at myself. The spirit spoke through me as I viewed what unfolded before me. It truly was an amazing experience. The temperature inside the cave was cool but acceptable. A granite table sat in the center of the cave. You would think it would have been uncomfortable to lie on, but I lay down on the stone table and found that it was very comfortable. Today, a beautiful greenish-yellow orb illuminated the space. The orb was a collective consciousness of spirits to teach and heal. The combination of colors within the light touched my heart center and distributed its light all around my body. I was being prepared to receive information, and then spirit me.

We come here to teach you to teach all of humanity. We have messages you must convey to everyone. With the insight you receive from this experience, and when you begin to apply what you have learned, you will begin to spread your wisdom with others by your words and and/or actions. We are all connected. You are all connected with each other as well as with us. Peace and harmony on earth cannot be achieved with us alone, we need your assistance to accomplish this.

It is time to start making positive changes within your life. It is time to stop the negative cycles, negative thought patterns, and negative actions toward yourself and others. It is time to focus your energy on love, compassion, forgiveness and seeing all as one. It is time to become one of love and understanding and to embrace the oneness of source energy within each other. It is challenging for the human to understand this and accept this to be true but once you begin to see love and light within all of creation and that all are connected and share source energy, then you will begin to understand your soul plan on a deeper level. This is not an easy task that we ask of you, but we are here to help you along the way.

Every moment of everyday, focus your attention and thoughts of being in the moment and appreciating all that surrounds you. Appreciate all those you interact with. Appreciate yourself and all your qualities and uniqueness. Appreciate all the things you experience. Become one within each moment in time and remember that all things are connected. When you find gratitude for all things, you will begin to see positive things happening and flow to you because you will have a deeper understanding that all is connected.

I sat upon the granite rock, then stood, placed my hands in prayer position, bowed my head, and exited the crystal cave. Once again, today's message was short and to the point.

Reflection on Day 3

As I reflected upon day three, I began to feel that there was a greater importance to all of the information conveyed than I originally realized. When I began this project, I thought I would just share the experiences I had each day that I meditated with these wings. However, now I was sensing that there was an urgency for us to learn—or relearn, rather—the importance of these topics that we might gain more understanding to help us on our own path and in the overall journey of the Harmony Movement.

Today's message was very straightforward and to the point once again. We need to reconnect with source energy, which is divine love, and we need to remember and respect that each of us holds that within us. We are all created of source energy, and we all hold divine love within us. Sometimes we forget that about ourselves and each other. We forget to love ourselves and each other as if we were part of this greater energy we call God, the creator of all things. We are part of that; we each hold that divine energy within us. This was a good reminder that we need to remember that in all we do. We need to respect and love ourselves and each other, because after all, we are all connected. We are all pieces of source energy.

We must move forward from our past lives, past mistakes and past repetition of negative actions and begin to forgive ourselves and others and heal the karma that will ultimately heal us. By doing so, we will heal the energy that surrounds us and that is within us, and then, in effect, we will begin to heal others. If you can find peace within yourself about things that you have done or things that others have done to you that caused you pain in any sort of way, then you can move past the block and the pain into the flow of where you need to go at this stage in your life. We are all here to learn, and we all make mistakes along the way. That is part of the learning. But we also need to learn from the mistakes we make and the mistakes others make, and then we have to decide to let those mistakes go with a better understanding that there is something greater overall for us to accomplish, which is finding divine love for all.

Action for Day 3

Take some quiet time and think about how you feel about yourself, and be honest about it. Try to forgive yourself for actions in the past that you are not proud of. See yourself as a divine being, part of the greater whole of what we call the Creator. Then see others as also being part of the divine. Take a few moments to surround yourself with divine love and light, and if you are able to, send love and light to those who have caused you pain or distress in the past as well. Journal your thoughts and the insights that come to you.

Journal for Day 3

_____

_____

_____

_____

_____

_____

_____

_____

_____

_____

_____

_____

_____

_____

_____

_____

_____

_____

_____

_____

_____

_____

_____

_____

~

You might wonder how I meditate with such a massive crystal. In general, I find it very easy to meditate with crystals. I have connected with crystals on a deep level for many years now, and I understand their language, I accept their healing, and I allow myself to be open to receiving the information that they provide to me. So as I sit in a chair next to this huge geode, I go into my quiet meditative state by placing one of my hands somewhere on the geode itself. Then I allow myself to relax and drift into the purple ray of the crystal cave as I begin my journey each time.

Today as I was preparing to meditate with these wings, I decided to give them a bath first. They were a little dusty, and of course you can only imagine how difficult it would be to keep all of these amethyst points clean. I find the easiest way is to put some distilled water in a spray bottle and apply it to sections of the wings. I use distilled water so it will not leave spots. Any negative energy that it might have absorbed is drained through its cracks at the bottom. Occasionally I also smudge sage or play crystal singing bowls near the geode as well, just to refresh its energy that way. All of these methods cleanse, recharge, and reset its energies.

The geode also has a beautiful white aura surrounding it, which I have captured on video (see video still on page 38). It has an angelic feel to it, and it radiates its beautiful energy to fill the complete space that it occupies.

After the geode's little bath this morning, I felt the energy recharged and ready for a new meditative lesson. So let us begin.

Day 4

As soon as I placed my fingers on the amethyst, I was immediately taken into the crystal cave of the purple ray. Again, I saw myself wearing a flowing white dress, but this time I also had white flowers in my hair. For this session I decided to sit lotus style on the rock bed that I normally lay upon.

"I am open to receiving what information you are to give me today," I said. "But first I have a question. Can you tell me how old you are?"

Are you talking about the geode that you stepped into? If so, that is thousands of years old, and it hold thousands and thousands of years of information—past and future information as well as spiritual guidance. However, the spirit of us who speak through these wings—we are infinite, as you are too. There is no age with a soul. There is no age for spirit. It is an infinite energy.

I felt the energy radiating from the crystal geode on my hand, and it traveled through my body as I was in this meditative state. "Could you please provide me with what information I must share today?"

Since we have already spoken of the infinite, that is the topic of today. Energy is infinite. We are all energy: you are energy, all earthly things and creation are energy, all of the universe is energy. And it is all-infinite, everlasting, ever-expanding, ever-growing, ever-changing energy. You have just barely begun to tap into the resources and the information at your fingertips, so to speak. Everyone has the ability to tap into this energy and information, and there are no limits. It is so vast that it is hard for the human to comprehend how much they are capable of achieving, doing, or obtaining. It is important to understand that you are infinite beings and to accept all the infinite wisdom and abundance that you are capable of holding. You already hold it. You just do not believe that you hold all of this because of your human experience and the time of human birth transition—the transition of coming into the human form is when you forgot all that you know. If you can train your human mind to believe that you hold all abundance and wisdom, then you are on the right track. Then you will begin to see many positive changes, and you will begin to radiate energy to others that lack that understanding. Just by believing that you hold this information, you will see it with your human eyes, and you will experience it with your physical being. You will come to completely understand it just by believing and trusting that this is to be so and that this is true.

It does not matter what level of understanding you are on; just try this challenge, and see what happens. Each day take some time and tell yourself that you are an infinite being filled with infinite wisdom and abundance, and believe what you tell yourself. That is the difficult part for many of you: believing what you tell yourself. Tell yourself this each day for thirty days.

When you start to believe that you are an infinite being filled with infinite wisdom and abundance, you will begin to see the changes and experience vast amounts of goodness that multiply over and over again, and you will start to radiate that energy to others as well. Others may not be aware or understand what you have learned; they might not be able to comprehend what you have achieved, but they will start to feel the energy radiating from you because you have come to an understanding that you are an infinite being of energy filled with wisdom and abundance. Just by your experiencing this truth, the energy that expands out from you will affect others in a positive way. You will be emitting positive pure energy and light, and you will touch others in a way that helps them. The more that others experience true understanding of wisdom and abundance, the better, because it spreads like a blanket around the human population, which allows more and more people to awaken and come to this realization. The ultimate goal of every soul is to learn all they are capable of: divine love, understanding, and acceptance of all that is positive and pure at all times.

All life and spirit are infinite but the human places restrictions upon themselves in the form of time. There is no time in the universe; time was created by the human, and from our standpoint, it has been regarded as something that holds you back. If you forget about timelines and adhering to time for a moment, and you function by sensing and paying attention to the information that is presented to you, then time will no longer be a factor or priority. You will do what is needed when needed, and you will have the understanding that everything is as it should be at all times. When there is no restriction of time, you come to the realization that everything is infinite.

"Thank you. I find this a little confusing myself, but maybe as I reflect on it for the rest of the day, I can make more sense of it and convey it to my readers in such a way that makes sense. Will you help me do that?"

Yes. You will take our energy with you as you reflect upon these words that we told you. We will give you the insight of what you need to say.

"Thank you so very much."

I bowed my head, I put my hands in prayer position, and I walked out of the amethyst cave backward into the light of the day.

Reflection on Day 4

As I sat and reflected on day four, I felt grateful for the information that was coming forth to help us with our own individual journeys. We are taught quite often to speak positively, think positively, and that what we say and what we speak are what we become. We are also taught that we are infinite beings. Putting those two concepts together seems to be a little challenging at times. Trying to understand and see ourselves as infinite beings is a challenge. Many people think that their life is just this period of time on earth, and then it ends. However, we are infinite beings; we continually grow and learn from past lives, in this life and on to the next.

Our human experience is just a little speck of time in our complete existence. There is no time in the universe. Humans created the perception of time in the earthly realm, and having done so, we now live our human lives around time. Time constricts us in so many ways. If we can forget the concept of time for a moment and focus on our infinite energy that holds all universal wisdom, I am sure it can lead to remarkable things. That sounds kind of uncertain, doesn't it? To say to yourself that you hold all infinite wisdom, but I believe that to be true. I believe that we have just forgotten it while we are here. I find that we question ourselves and our capabilities so much that we forget to trust what information spirit has given us.

Also, I have been told many times in the past that there is enough abundance for everyone on this planet. It is just ego, greed, and fear that limit us from obtaining what we wish to have. If we can train our mind to think in such a way, and believe it when we say we are infinite beings filled with infinite wisdom and abundance, I think that we will experience some amazing things in our near future. I believe we are also just barely tapping into our full potential. I have no doubt the future holds great understanding.

Action for Day 4

Write the affirmation "I am an infinite being of wisdom and abundance" on several sticky notes, and place them around your home and workspace, in your purse or wallet, and anywhere else that you will see them often. Say these words out loud several times a day for thirty days as suggested by the geode spirits. You can take it a step further and focus on what you are saying by closing your eyes and truly listening to your words. Visualize yourself as an infinite being of wisdom and abundance, and picture in your mind what that would look like to you. Journal any thoughts or insights that come to you when you say that affirmation for the first time. Then check back in thirty days and see if you feel differently about the statement, and if things have shifted in a positive direction for you since you first began to say it each day.

Journal for Day 4

Day 5

As I prepared myself to go into the purple crystal cave, I wondered what the next lesson would be. Every time I entered the cave, it was so very peaceful, and it was as if I had stepped into an actual crystal cave. Looking within the cave, I saw that the walls were surrounded with deep-purple amethyst points, the floor was of dirt, and a carved granite stone bed sat in the center. This was the stone that I saw myself either sitting or lying upon during the experience. The room was illuminated from a light source, but I did not know where that light came from. It was the most brilliant color of purple I had ever seen. The energy was very calm and peaceful.

To begin the day's experience, I placed my hand upon the geode wings and let myself drift into the crystal cave.

I saw myself walking into the cave and stopping at the entrance, looking around to get my bearings. I wore a flowing white dress as always, and I was barefoot so that I could connect more fully. I went to the granite bed at the center of the cave, and today I as lay down, I lay down and asked the spirit to please share with me what I needed to know today. "Please," I said, "if you will, tell me what I need to know today. What do I need to share with others?"

As I held this crystal, I immediately felt the grand energy going into my hand and up my arm as a beautiful pulsating energy source.

We are pleased that you are dedicating time to working with us. There is much to be shared, and there is much that we want others to know. There is much that we want to clarify for those who are uncertain.

As I saw myself lying in the cave, accepting the words that the spirits provided, there was a white orb floating in the space above me, and it was the most brilliant white light I had ever seen. "Who is that with us?" I asked.

This is the universal white light; this is the pure light; this is all that is love and light. It is here so you can see it for yourself. We tell you about such things, but we want you to experience it for yourself so you can convey firsthand knowledge of the experience. We want you to know that you are all capable of experiencing connection at this level. You are all capable of experiencing divine love. You are all capable of experiencing the eternal and infinite wisdom that we spoke of yesterday. You are all capable of shining your light upon this earth, and when all humankind shines their light, earth will be in harmony once again, as it was in the beginning. You are all capable of achieving and experiencing deep peace within and obtaining understanding of why you are here and what you need to do to accomplish your goals to move to the next level of enlightenment.

"How do we go about that?" I asked.

Find the white light that pulses within, that unites your soul with pure universal love. Each and every one of you has it at the very core of your being. Find that within yourself, and follow it. It will take you where you need to go. You must follow with it with your heart and trust that you are following what you need to follow.

"How do we find that within us?" I asked again.

You must love yourself first and foremost, for all that you are and all that you will be and all that you have been. You have forgotten who you are, and that is the root of the problem with most humans. You have forgotten who you are, you have forgotten to take care of yourself, you have forgotten to love yourself, and you have forgotten what you are capable of. The first step is to love yourself unconditionally, including your physical being, your soul, your experiences, and your knowledge of everything associated with you. You must love you. Next, you must forgive yourself of anything that you have felt guilt over and release it and let it go so that it can help you find the love for yourself. You must have an understanding of what you have endured and learned in this lifetime. You must have an understanding of why you have experienced the things that you have. Go deep within, and connect to all that you are to accomplish this.

"It seems simple enough but from the human standpoint it feels like it is something that is challenging to us."

You must connect to source energy often. This can be achieved through meditation, connection to nature, or spending quiet moments in reflective thought. Every soul, every person is created from source energy. Everyone carries source energy within them. When you come upon the earthly plane, you are given the choices of how you wish to express yourself, how you wish to learn, how you wish to understand, how you wish to relate to others, and how you wish to react to things that might happen to you. Follow your heart deep down inside. We are not talking about the emotional part of your being; we are talking about your intuition, which is your internal guidance system from your soul. Follow it deep down inside, and it will always lead you to where you need to go.

You must rediscover yourself and find who you really are and let your true inner light shine. Love yourself unconditionally, without hesitation or restriction. You must love yourself unconditionally and forgive yourself for anything that you felt bad about in your past. It is time to accept that what has happened has happened and to move on from it.

If you stay stuck dwelling upon past experiences that might not have been ideal, then you will not move forward within your own learning experience. You will stay stuck in that cycle. You must be willing to let those things go. We were with you and we have helped you in your preplanning phase, in the soul space before you came to the earthly plane. You have a detailed plan and agenda of what this earthly life will be like for you in order for you to achieve certain learning experiences and find what you need to find to be able to move on to the next level in your own personal journey.

The goal, the ultimate goal, is to ascend into eternal light. Once you achieve complete divine love, that is when you ascend, and you will be a master to help others along their paths. Divine love means to love yourself and each other person and/or soul unconditionally, regardless of their actions upon earth. This is very difficult for many to achieve, and that is why it takes so many lifetimes of learning to find this understanding.

We are hoping with this experience, and that by your spending time with us, something might ignite a flame or turn on a switch or give somebody something that they can relate to or understand in such a way that they might change their thought process so they are no longer held back from their past or by a lack of self-love. It is our hope that something mentioned here will bring about motivation to see things differently to help them climb the next step in their own personal direction.

That is enough for today; you are feeling depleted, because this is a heavy topic. Rest, reflect, and conserve your energy for our next discussion.

I felt the powerful energy continue to pulsate through me as the channeled information come through. My body vibrated, and I did not quite understand exactly what the spirits were saying. As I prepared myself to exit the cave, I sat up and grounded myself with my bare feet on the dirt. And as I did so, the brilliant white orb that was floating above me burst into a ray of white light and illuminated the cave with such grandeur that I was in awe. I felt waves of love, peace, and protection in ways that I had not felt before. I wished to hold this in my heart always.

I stood and put my hands in prayer position, bowed my head, gave thanks, and exited the cave, walking backward into reality. As I finished this meditation, I pulled my hand off the geode and found it was actually pulsating and vibrating, the energy was so intense.

Reflection on Day 5

As I reflected on the information provided for day five, I was overwhelmed. I am not even sure where to begin, so it is probably best to break it down into parts.

First the spirits were talking about being capable, because we forget how capable we really are. We are capable of experiencing a deep connection with spirit, learning from spirit, and experiencing divine love and infinite wisdom. We are all capable of achieving peace and understanding of why we are here. To do that we must reconnect with who we really are, and we must find ourselves. Reconnecting with who we really are is reconnecting with source energy. I see it as one and the same. When you reconnect with who you really are, you can receive profound inner guidance and wisdom.

The spirits also touched on finding self-love, on loving yourself divinely without conditions, restrictions, and judgment. Love everything about yourself, and forgive anything that you have done in the past that you are not proud of or that has caused you distress in some way. We all had a plan coming to this earth to accomplish specific goals, and much of the experiences we have gone through are part of the plan.

We must also focus on finding divine love: that means to love all of creation without condition. That is the ultimate goal of all of these lifetimes of learning and lessons and trials and tribulations. It is not an easy task, and that is why we choose to return for more life experiences time and time again, to learn more lessons for us to get us closer to experiencing divine love. Some have accomplished this and have become ascended masters; once we have learned everything we need to learn, we will also become ascended masters. Some of us will have many more lifetimes of learning before we reach that level, but each lifetime we learn something more, and if we apply what we have learned, it gets us that much closer.

Action for Day 5

Take some time to either meditate or spend time in nature or in quiet thought to connect with your higher self and ask who you really are. Listen to the answers that come to you.

Also, look in the mirror and appreciate yourself. Smile at your reflection, and tell yourself, "I love you." Do it often until you feel comfortable with yourself. Consider reading Louise Hay's book *Mirror Work* for in-depth self-love techniques. Journal how it felt to say I love you to yourself. Did you struggle with it? Did it feel unnatural or did it feel right?

If you are ready to move even deeper, focus on some past issues you have been holding on to, and let them go. Find peace and forgiveness for those issues or experiences, and come to terms with them. This process can take time so do not rush it. Not everyone is ready for that step, but if you are feeling that you are, take that step and heal the past. I would suggest you journal all thoughts, visions, or anything else that comes to you during your quiet time.

Journal for Day 5

_____

_____

_____

_____

_____

_____

_____

_____

_____

_____

_____

_____

_____

_____

_____

_____

_____

_____

_____

_____

_____

_____

_____

_____

Journal for Day 5

~

You might be wondering if I do these meditations on consecutive days. I do not. There are some days when energetically I am just not able to go in such deep or channeled meditations. It is important to pay attention to your physical body when going into deep meditations. I do meditate every single day, but on the days when I am not physically feeling I can handle going in deeply, I just focus on being at peace and on my own well-being. So I meditate with these amethyst wings whenever I feel the energy is right. Plus I do not want to rush the process. I want it to flow as it is meant to flow.

I have no idea what to expect each time I meditate with these wings, and each time it is a unique experience. That is what makes it exciting as well, and just tapping into such a deep realm is so exciting and so wonderful, and I feel so very privileged and honored to be able to do so. Everyone is capable of doing this if they spend some time and practice deep meditation.

I do go about meditation with this geode differently than I do with my other crystals. My typical meditation routine with crystals is to lay down in my bed with crystals either on or around my body, or I hold them during the meditation. This particular crystal is too large for me to hold, of course, because it is nearly six hundred pounds. I have to go to it; it cannot come to me. I sit in a reclining chair next to these wings, because that seems to be the easiest way to be able to touch them while I am in a meditative state.

Are you ready to continue on?

Day 6

Before I proceeded into meditation for this day, I wondered what the wings could possibly want to say today. So as I prepared for day six, I sat in the chair beside the wings and put my fingers inside the geode so I was touching the amethyst points, and I let myself drift into the purple-ray cave once again.

As I stepped into the entrance of the cave, I noticed that I was surrounded by angels. I rarely see angels in my meditative state; I hear them, feel them, and see them as energy, but I rarely see them as what we typically perceive them to look like. This time I saw them. There was an abundance of angels surrounding me in this place as I stepped into the cave. The space was literally filled with angels, and it was so beautiful. They were all different and radiated different universal light colors, such as blue, purple, yellow, and white. It was a most glorious energy to experience, and I saw myself standing inside the entrance of the cave. I was in awe of all the angelic beauty reflecting the light on the purple points of the amethyst.

I stepped farther into the cave, and I sat upon my rock bed at the center of the cave, just taking in all of the beauty around me. I felt such a very deep state of peace.

We show you these angels today so you are reminded that your angels are always with you. Your spirit guides and your angels travel wherever you go, and you have more than what you realize or have been taught in the past. You are surrounded by thousands of angels everywhere you go. To put it in perspective, think of each person that you encounter, and imagine that they are surrounded by thousands of angels as well. So there are millions of angels in a place that has several people, because you multiply all of the people that are located in a space times a thousand, and that is how many angels are within that space as well. They are there to help your every need and want. Everyone has one main guardian angel, but the rest are there if need be. They are thrilled about what you are learning and that you know about them. They are filled with joy when you ask them for help and guidance.

"I have been aware of my angel and spirit guides for some time," I said, "and I always asked the angels and archangels for assistance, but I did not really have a clear vision of how many angels there truly were. Now that I see such an abundance of angels in this space alone, I have a better understanding of how many angels are really truly with me at all times. Thank you for this visual."

As I lay down on my rock bed and got settled in, I closed my eyes and was ready to accept what information was given.

Today we are taking you on a trip, and we will teleport you on this beautiful journey to where we want you to go. The angels are experts at teleporting, so they will lead the way as we begin this journey.

Teleportation is the action of being transported across a space or distance in an instant. This can be accomplished through hypnosis, deep meditation, or the dream state. It does take time and practice to achieve this type of experience, but it can be done.

I had no idea where I was headed, but it appeared as if we were on a train, and it was moving so fast that the landscape went by too quickly for me to distinguish anything but streaks of colors as we went by. It was all a blur of color passing me by.

Today we take you to paradise. This is a long-forgotten place that is now preserved for those who are capable of handling the trip and of respecting this place.

We stopped, and I felt myself floating down as my feet touched the ground to where we landed in this beautiful place. It was a very magical. It was filled with sparkling, unearthly beauty. It was not something I remembered seeing on earth before, but deep down in my heart, I knew that I had been at such a place before. This was a place of preserved beauty and harmony for all creatures who are here.

I was at a small section of this vast place the spirits referred to as paradise, and I had to agree this was what I saw in my mind as paradise. In front of me, I there was a pool of water being filled from a waterfall that sparkled like diamonds, and in the pool of water, dolphins were playing and singing their beautiful song in harmony with the birds that flew above. I saw flowers of every shape and color imaginable, and their fragrance was divine. The trees and shrubs were brilliant shades of greens, with other complementary colors. A doe gently walked up to the pond and took a drink. She looked up and saw me watching her, and I felt a smile appear through her dark eyes, and I smiled back as we came to an understanding of respect for one another.

Everywhere I looked there was a deep, rich beauty, and each sound was peaceful and calming. The sky was a deep, rich blue, and everything was alive with passion for what it was. This was truly a magical place. There was no one there but me at the moment. As I moved about and explored, I saw birds flying in the sky and butterflies fluttering around. I found a beautiful flat rock in the nearby meadow, and I sat upon the rock, looking at all the mountains and hills in the distance. I listened to the laughter of the dolphins playing in the pond nearby, and I felt a big smile appear on my face.

I was filled with gratitude in my heart to be able to experience this. I was appreciative to be in the moment in this sliver of time. Nothing else mattered during this moment as I accepted all the beautiful gifts that I had been given to experience this amazing wonder. This was a very special place, and it truly was paradise.

There was other wildlife such as deer, rabbits, and squirrels nearby, and I saw large animals such as elephants and lions in the distance. They were all in harmony with their environment and each other.

Everything was in harmony. There was no competition, no hierarchy, and no ego. It was all pure beauty, pure love, and respect for each other's souls, whether it be animal, plant, or human. Everything here had a universal understanding that they were all one.

It was such a beautiful experience, and I was so very grateful to have seen it. "Where is this place now?" I asked.

This is what it used to be on earth for all life forms before the ego, greed, and corruption occurred. All those on the path of enlightenment are helping restore harmony on earth, whether they know it or not. The more that you open your heart to beauty and love, the closer you will come to this beautiful place once again. You will not see it in your particular physical lifetime this time around. However, it is getting closer and closer than it has been in many, many thousands of years. It is on the right track, and we are overall very pleased with the progress.

Paradise is within each of you and each of you can access it when you are in alignment with your soul path. You just need to find it and see for yourself. Then you will begin to believe once again that you are surrounded by beauty.

I was immediately teleported back to the cave and saw myself on the rock from which I had begun. I still lay there in a meditative state, but I was looking down upon myself. "Is there anything else that I need to share today?" I asked.

Every time that you experience a transformation cycle, it is worth all the challenges and all the difficulty that you endure to get to eternal and soul wisdom. It is there, it is hidden deep within your soul, and it is coming forth little by little. Each challenge that you learn from and conquer brings you one more piece of eternal wisdom that is all stored deeply within your soul. Each time you recognize that you have learned something from a challenging experience, you have become that much closer to your eternal wisdom. Accessing your eternal wisdom will help you find paradise.

I sat up from the stone bed and stood, bowed my head, put my hands in prayer position, and walked out of the cave, giving deep gratitude and thanks for this amazing experience.

Reflection on Day 6

I had known for some time that angels surround us and that they are always there when we need them, but not to the magnitude that I was shown today. It was refreshing to me to know that there were countless angels surrounding us every day.

I experienced teleportation during meditation a few years ago. It is an exciting way to travel and get to destinations quickly. Everyone is capable of experiencing this, but I want to be realistic here and mention that it is not something that seems to happen easily. I think it is best to really get a good foundation down for deep meditation, and then teleportation can be achieved if you set your intentions on it. Keep in mind that you may need to practice it before you get the feel of how to achieve it.

The destination of today's journey was the most amazing place I have ever seen in this lifetime. The colors were so rich and vibrant, and the overall feel of that place they called paradise was absolutely beyond amazing.

It felt like everything was in order and harmony. It felt peaceful, and each component was respected and understood as being an important part of the whole. I think we all have a different opinion of what paradise would look like, but I think we can all agree that it would be a place where we would all feel in harmony with each other. When we begin to become balanced and re-aligned with who we are and find a state of peace, then I feel that we can access paradise. What we think of "paradise" can be different for each of us, but we all hold that within the depths of who we are. It is there awaiting us to uncover the layers of enlightenment.

It was a wonderful experience, and I am grateful they shared it with us.

Action for Day 6

Find a quiet place where you can be comfortable and undisturbed for a bit of time. Close your eyes, and visualize thousands of angels surrounding you. See what they look like to you. Notice their shape, their features, their colors, and their overall energy. Take a moment to ask the angels to assist you with something you need help with in your life right now, and remember to thank them.

Then think about the journey to paradise. Ask the angels to help you travel to paradise, and see what that looks like to you. Notice the sounds, colors, and overall feel of the place you visit. It will be different and unique for everyone. You may want to journal your experiences and thoughts that come to you.

Journal for Day 6

~

Before I went into the meditation for the day, I felt I needed to share the insight of what came to me regarding frequency and energy. After meditations I quite often get insight on things that just are downloaded to me automatically. It is as if I go through the meditation process and receive information at that time, but as I am still open to receiving after that, so I quite often continue to receive information throughout the following day and night. I had much debate with myself on even providing this insight because it is rather confusing but my guidance kept prompting me to share it, so here it is.

Everything is energy, and all energy has a frequency. First we need a clear understanding of what frequency and energy is. The definition of energy is "the ability to be active" and "usable power." The definition of frequency is "the rate at which something occurs or is repeated over a particular period of time, or the rate at which a vibration occurs that constitutes a wave." I think it is easier to think of frequency as the waves of the energy. So for example, if you are experiencing a negative situation (negative energy), then the frequency are the waves radiating from that energy which are sending out negative vibrations such as fear, worry or stress. If you are operating at a lower frequency than that of your energy, then naturally your energy is going to be lowered as well, so things will be sluggish. That is when you will experience the lower energy vibration, such as stress, worry, fear, pain, illness, and so on. When you are at a higher frequency, your energy level is at a higher level as well, and that is when you are in the state of joy, happiness, and gratitude. When you are challenged with negative situation (lower energy), it is best to keep your energy high. That is the challenge for many. You can change your frequency even though you experience a lower (negative) energy. You can bring that frequency up by changing your thought process and your attitude about the situation. Then you change the energy to a higher level, and the vibration continues at a higher level. It is imperative to maintain the higher-level vibration frequency and energy at all times. It is our natural state to function at a higher frequency and energy, however; it is when we allow negative situations to affect us that lowers our energy to the negative state.

The frequency of a situation can be amplified or diffused depending on how you respond. If you respond to a negative situation in a negative manner (anger, fear, doubt, worry, etc.) then the frequency of the negative energy will amplify and continue on. If you respond to a negative situation in a positive manner (peace, love, kindness, forgiveness, compassion, etc.) then the negative energy will be diffused.

For example, if you experience anger because of something that was said, than you are responding to the frequency waves of the energy source that angered you. The waves of the energy traveled toward you which in turn made you angry. If you continue to feel anger, then the frequency waves will continue on through you out to others. Others will feel the effects of your anger. If you find a way to deal with the anger you felt and return to a state of peace, then you will emit peaceful frequency waves out from then on, so the anger waves will have been diffused.

I know this is a confusing topic to get but I do not think we should get caught up on the terms frequency or energy. I think it is probably more important to understand that it makes a difference how we respond to situations. If we can return to a state of peace and maintain it after experiencing a negative occurrence, it will be easier to diffuse the negative energy you may have experienced from that occurrence and return back to a state of peace within. I am curious if the spirits will weigh in on this topic.

Day 7

So as I prepared myself to meditate with the purple wings on day seven, I wondered what the topic of the day would be. Would it be something along the lines of frequency and energy? Would it be another teleportation journey? I never know what to expect until I am in that deep state of meditation. Day six's journey was magical and beautiful in so many ways, and I hope that you enjoyed coming along with me. Now you know that there is true paradise within all of us; we just have to tap into it—and remember, all of us are capable of doing that.

I sat in the recliner next to the wings, and I placed my hands inside them on the points of the amethyst. I closed my eyes and took a few deep breaths, and I let myself drift into the purple ray of the crystal cave. I was immediately taken into the cave. I stepped inside and stopped at the entrance to look around, and I saw the beautiful purple illumination of color radiating from the points of the crystal wall. It was the most beautiful shade of purple. It was so very calming and peaceful each time that I stepped into this purple ray. I felt deeply honored to be part of this beautiful experience, and to be able to share this with others. I stepped inside and walked toward the granite bed. I sat there for a moment with my hands beside my body, resting on the granite. The granite was very grounding, and I understood that I needed to be grounded at the same time during these meditative sessions, because the powerful energy from this huge crystal could be overwhelming if I were not grounded at the same time. I lay upon the granite stone, and I immediately felt myself floating about six inches above it. I was levitating in a horizontal position.

Anything and everything is possible. So many times you have to experience something to believe it to be true or to have complete understanding of the reason for the experience. So many times you have to experience something to learn what you need to learn because just being told about some of such things does not often convince you. But if you experience something firsthand and learn from it, then you have this absolute knowing that it is true and that you are capable of doing it again, as well as, the reason for the experience and how it relates to your soul path.

When you come to earth in the human form, you have this cloud upon you, and you forget all of these things that you are relearning right now. You know all these things deep within; you are just relearning it or uncovering it, so to speak. You are relearning all of the universal knowledge that you hold deep within your being. You are relearning your path and your true self, step by step, each moment of every day. When you come to earth in the physical form as a baby, you forget everything that you had known from before. You forget the conversations and the planning in the soul space prior to your earth birth, as well as your other lifetimes, other worlds, and how truly connected you are to the entire universe.

Although many young children do have somewhat of a memory of such things, they quickly forget because of cultural and societal influence and human disapproval of accepting and expanding the universal wisdom. It is the current culture that finds it displeasing, so in most cases, it is seen to be untruth. Therefore children are taught that such information is not correct, and then that influences their beliefs as they grow older. Many of you have been influenced this way, but now you are relearning your truth. You come into this earthly plane, and you forget or are exposed to different opinions that mask the truth of who you really are. Many of you on the path to relearn your truth, and you will be helping the greater whole to find harmony and peace upon this earthly plane once again. It will in fact take many generations before that is achieved, but we believe that you are capable of continuing this path of peace and enlightenment and helping others to find it in order to achieve the whole world's return to a state of peace once again.

"What do we need to do now in order to help this endeavor?"

It is so very important to be your true authentic self at all times. Then your true inner being will shine its light; your truth will shine its light. Then you will show others that it is preferable to be yourself. Others need to learn that it is good to be their true selves at all times. That is the most imperative objective at the moment: to learn to be yourself at all times. Do not judge one another. Find forgiveness for yourself and others, and strive to have universal love at all times.

Of course, we ask a lot of you, and we understand that in the human form, you have forgotten all of these things. Some of you will continue to be caught in the cycles of disbelief and negative vibration, but you will eventually break that cycle and catch up to where you need to be. Others will question if they are ready to do these things because of the effects of fear, ego, and negative vibrations from culture and society, and they will continue to hide from their own truth. Yet on the other hand, there are a grand number of you who are on this path and who are willing to learn, grow, expand, and trust what knowledge you are obtaining. You are the ones who will help the rest by your actions of compassion, kindness, and love, which in essence is being your true self.

The life experience can be difficult and challenging at times, but you are given challenges because that is part of your learning process, and knowing these things that we share with you should help you. The more you can get through the challenging times with a loving heart, the easier it will become to address in the future, and you will be a role model for others who are going through similar challenges but have not yet found the inner truth or knowledge that you have.

"Thank you for the information. But I have a question. May I ask, if you please? Yesterday I was given a download of information regarding frequency and energy. Is there anything you can add to that?"

Yes. Frequency is as constant as energy is. Although you consider frequency and energy different things in the earthly sense, they are quite similar in the universal sense. Everything has a frequency, and everything is energy. It is easier if you see the two as different components of the whole.

If you are affected by a negative energy, your frequency will be depleted, and vice versa—if you are affected by a lower frequency, your energy will be depleted. You will need to raise your frequency and your energy to reduce the negative impact that is caused. How do you do that, you might ask? Always hold your joy, happiness, and gratitude at all times, regardless of what experiences are *happening, either global or individual. Do not let yourself get caught up in negative situations that are occurring, because then you fall victim to those situations, and then you will have to try to obtain a higher frequency and energy once again.*

The longer that you hold a higher frequency and energy, the less likely that you will fall into the negative state for any reason. If you do, it will not last long, because you will be able to pull yourself out more quickly.

They are all connected: frequency, vibration, and energy. It is all one as well, just as you are all individuals but at the same time are also all one. So you are affected by other individuals' actions, but it is up to you if you want to be affected in such a way that depletes your energy, and it is up to you if you remain positive. If you remain positive in the worst of times, you will build up your frequency and energy levels so that it will be easier to maintain those levels. Just as you are downloading and channeling all this information, you are on a very high frequency to accept all of the information you are given. Those who are on lower frequency are not able to hear, see, or feel the spirits that surround them. When you are on a higher frequency, you have opened yourself up to allow yourself to receive the positive energy that is around you.

"Thank you so much." As I sat up, I felt overwhelmed with information, and I would have to process it during the next day or so. I stood up, put my hands in prayer position, bowed my head, and walk backward out of the cave into the sunlight. I turned and faced the sun, and I smiled.

That was a very intense and informative session. My hand throbbed with energy from holding the crystal as long as I had for this meditation. I needed to take a rest, and then I would take a moment to review what had been said and to come up with conclusions about what had been discussed today.

Reflection on Day 7

There was so much information given during day seven's session that I feel that it could be overwhelming.

First of all they spoke of how when we came to this life on earth, we came here with a cloud of what we know to be true. As we grow from child to adult, we are influenced greatly by culture, society, and familial beliefs. That intensifies the cloud that hides the knowledge that we hold within ourselves. It is important to focus on being our true selves, which are reflections of the divine. When we are our true selves, we feel and reflect divine love, and that can impact others in a profound and positive way. We have just begun to uncover all the knowledge that we forgot when we transitioned into human form for this life experience. As we relearn what we have forgotten, we are transformed into a continuous state of love, compassion, and truth.

I can see how energy and frequency are tied to this subject. As we maintain a positive energy and frequency, more positive energy and frequency will radiate toward us. It will be a continuous flow of the positive. That will help our overall objective: to find our innermost truth and divine love. So when we say positive energy or negative energy, I believe it is easier to understand it as a form of power. The frequency is the vibration of the power and its amplification. So for example, when negative energy has occurred, quite often the media will amplify that energy by stating what occurred (something such as war or a natural disaster like an earthquake), and thousands of others react in a negative way by repeating it, gossiping about it, inflating or distorting the facts, and creating fear because of it. That negative energy has just been amplified, causing the frequency to intensify in a negative manner. Frequency can be carried on for days, weeks, or even years depending on how much power that energy has increased. If thousands or even millions of people were responding in a negative way to a negative situation, can you see how the energy from that situation could be amplified? All of those people's vibrations are contributing to the frequency of that negative occurrence. If many were to react in a positive way, to state peaceful things, or to pray or help in some way, then that would counteract the frequency of that negative energy.

I do not think we really need to get caught up in the words energy and frequency so much, but I do believe that it is important to maintain a higher level of positive energy and frequency at all times.

In other words, we should keep our thoughts and words positive on a high level at all times. Many people are affected by the words and actions of others, so if you maintain the higher energy and frequency, then that will help us to break the cycles of negative energy and continue on the path that unfolds as we advance in our learning and expand our forgotten knowledge of who we really are.

Action for Day 7

Think about your own transformation, how you are unfolding the hidden wisdom from within, and what that means to you.

Do you think that your thoughts, words, and actions affect others in any way?

What does the statement "find your truth" mean to you?

What does it mean to you to be your true authentic self?

Does it frighten you to be your authentic self, or do you find it exciting?

Whichever way you answer that, why do you think you feel that way?

Also, think about how you react to negative situations. When you respond to a negative situation in a negative manner, how does that make you feel?

Journal any thoughts that may come to you. This is a heavy topic, so take your time with your own reflection on it.

Journal for Day 7

Day 8

I settled in my chair, got relaxed, and took a few deeps breaths. I tended to go deeply into the meditation with this geode rather quickly because it is a very big piece and is very powerful. I set my hand upon the points of the crystal on the lower side of one of the wings. It was the easiest place for me to place my hand for the duration of the meditation. I reclined in my chair, got comfortable, closed my eyes, and began my journey once again.

I immediately started to feel the vibration of the crystal on my fingertips, going down my hand and surrounding my arm, and within a few moments, the vibration surrounded my whole body, and I felt the beautiful energy of this crystal throughout my being. It felt wonderful, but it could be draining, as I had experienced in past sessions. Any channeling session or deep guidance session can be draining. It is as if the spirits use my body as a conduit, as a channel to say what needs to be said, so my physical form actually experiences fatigue because of it. I quite often need to ground myself when I am finished with these types of meditative sessions, and I also need to be mindful of how I feel before and after I do these meditations.

I felt the crystal energy enter into my being as I stepped up to the entrance of the cave of the purple ray of the amethyst once again. I always saw myself from a distance in these meditations, looking from above or across the space. I always seemed to be wearing the same flowing white gown. It was a simple dress that touched the ground and flowed as I walked. It was short sleeved and conservative, and once again I had a ring of flowers in my hair. They looked like a little crown of white daisies on my head.

I stepped inside the cave and walked toward the granite bed. I sat upon the granite for a moment to get settled in, and then I lay down with my hands at my sides. I closed my eyes and awaited the information that needed to come through today. This time there was no illuminating orb or other source of light; it was just the glorious purple ray within the space. It seemed quieter today than normal—not that the other days were not quiet, but it just had a much more peaceful feel overall for some reason. I saw my angel floating above me, and I had the sense that there were many more spirits here than who had been speaking recently. Up to this point, only the masculine-feminine version of Andromeda had been speaking.

It has been several days since you have come here to be with us. We would appreciate it if you attempted to come more often. We have much to say.

This was not the first time that the spirits have had to set me straight when it came to working with them. They had a lot to convey to us, and I apparently had not been focused on the task at hand.

"I do apologize. May I ask, what is your message today?"

Peace. When you feel such profound and deep peace within yourself, you know all the answers. You can heal every part of your physicalness; everything can be healed once you are at a state of peace. If you maintain that state of peace, you will maintain that level of health physically and mentally. You will also maintain the gateway to wisdom and all that is. When you hold a peaceful state within your being, you know all that is, you know what needs to be accomplished, you know the ways to accomplish what needs to be accomplished, you know how to heal yourself, and you know how to spread the light and love to others. You will find there is no more urgency, confusion, uncertainty, stress, worry, or fear. You let the things go that do not matter.

Today we brought you here to experience that deep peacefulness. The more that you experience peace, and the more that you practice your ways of finding peace, and the more you maintain a peaceful being, the better you will be able to achieve all that you need and want to within this life cycle. You will be in a state of understanding what your personal path is all about. You will also understand how you are connected with others. You will understand the connection with who comes into your life and who leaves your life and why. You will understand the lessons that are presented to you, and you will understand how to master all things that seem challenging with ease. The more that you maintain this peaceful state, the more that you can handle all that comes your way with grace.

It is important that you realize how significant it is to maintain a state of peace. Then you will also radiate that vibration out into the world, and when more of you radiate that vibration out into the world, it will affect others in a profound way. They might not even realize what is happening, but you will affect others in a very positive way, and they will start to fall into the peaceful vibration that you emit. The more practice this, the more it will affect the earth—not only the people upon the earth, but every living thing upon the earth, and the earth herself. It is another step into the direction of ultimate harmony and unity.

You may question how to go about that. Go within; close your eyes, take a few deep breaths, and focus upon your soul and who you really are. Surround yourself with universal divine light. Reconnect with your source energy. So many times humans forget that they have a soul, they forget who they really are, they forget what they are capable of, and they forget all that is. It is really simple: just reconnect and find peace with who you are, and most importantly, accept who you are. Love who you are. Forgive yourself for what you might have accomplished in the past that you are not proud of. Let guilt dissolve. Take quiet time each day several times a day, and go within. Meditate. Connect and reconnect with all that you are and all that is, because you are one with source energy; you are oneness with all creation and God.

"I do not think that we realize how important it is that we practice finding peace within ourselves on a daily basis," I said. "I think we forget because we have, or we feel we have, so many earthly obligations to attend to each day. I think we forget because we have all of these obligations, and we put so much pressure upon ourselves that we forget what is truly important within our own path."

This is true. In your human experience, you forget what is important on a daily basis. Sometimes you are reminded of what is important when tragedy strikes, or when there is danger, or something along those lines. You have got to be in a constant awareness of what is important at all times, and being at a peaceful state at all times is very important.

Say perhaps you are being affected, or you are worried about being affected, by a particular occurrence. Worrying will not help anything, but it will continue to feed negative vibrations and amplify that energy out into the atmosphere. If you are worried about a certain occurrence, then you must go within and find peace and resolution about what is causing that worried state to occur within you. Then you can focus on stopping that fear, and when you stop that fear, at that point it will no longer radiate from you, but you will radiate peace in its place.

As a collective group radiating peace, this can be an accelerated earth-healing experience. So when people focus on peace regardless of the situation, they will affect somebody else, and more and so on. The more you focus on peace, the more at harmony your own being will become. Things that are pleasing to you will be more prevalent in your life, and you will experience more things that make you happy than you did before you were at a constant state of peacefulness. You will see things with a different viewpoint; you will see the world by looking through the eyes of your soul. You will be open to seeing the vast beauty right in front of you each and every moment. You will be in awe and wonder at all of the beautiful creations that surround you. That is when you become one within yourself and harmony with the one who created you.

When you find a state of peace and maintain it at a current vibration, your physical life will change and your spiritual life will accelerate, plus your karmas and your physical limitations will dissolve, and you will see that all things are possible. This benefits you in two ways. It benefits you personally in your physical being and soul path, but it also benefits others whom you are in contact with. It can be anybody you are in contact with, such as somebody walking by, an acquaintance, friend, family member, or loved one. If you maintain that state of peace, that will radiate to all of those you are in contact with, and so many of them need that within their own lives during this point of time. Just by helping yourself, you will help many, and the cycle will continue.

"Thank you for this information." I felt I must reflect upon this, because it had been a very intense session, and my whole body vibrated with the crystal ray. It was a very deep peacefulness, but at the same time, I felt the intense power of the urgency of their message today. I stood and walked backward with my head bowed and my hands in prayer position as I said thank you and walked out of the cave. Until next time. As I finalized this meditation, I removed my hand from the crystal, and my whole body was just singing with energy.

Reflection on Day 8

You would not think that discussing peace would be so intense, but it came through as being of great importance. This is not just something that we need to think about doing; it is something that the spirits really want us to focus on and maintain all the time. I always reach a deep state of peacefulness during meditation, but I find it difficult to focus on it throughout the day each day. I do find myself attempting to return to a more peaceful state after I have experienced stress in some way. I have no doubt that the more people that find the state of peace and maintain it often, the more others and Mother Earth will be affected in a very positive way as well.

This ties into yesterday's discussion of a collective whole which reacts to energy. If we all are in a state of positive, peaceful energy, then that will be amplified out to surround the whole world. The energy of peace will amplify and have a constant frequency that will continue flowing. Then everyone can live in harmony with all that is. Of course, our earthly experience does make it difficult at times to maintain a constant state of peace, but I think the more we at least try and the more we achieve it, the more it will help the greater overall consciousness of the planet. When we no longer experience stress, anger, worry, fear, or any other negative vibration, all of creation will be healed. Can you just imagine what it would be like if the whole world were at peace?

Action for Day 8

Try meditating each day to reach that state of peacefulness. If you are not used to meditation, start off with just a few minutes, and build from there. Those of you who struggle with meditation should check out my book *Meditation Made Easy Using Crystals* because it covers how you can achieve a peaceful state of meditation.

For those moments when you experience worry, stress, or any other negative energy, find a quiet place to close your eyes, take a few deep breaths, and then let your breathing return to a normal state. Surround yourself with beautiful divine love and light. Then focus on your innermost being and how beautiful and at peace it is. Feel the peace that surrounds you, and let yourself accept all the positive pure energy that encompasses you. Once you reach that state of peacefulness, either after meditation or a quick relaxation, hold that in your heart for the rest of the day.

If you are not able to spend time in meditation or a quick calming, just send yourself some peace, love, and light, and then send it out to the world as well.

After you have practiced reaching a state of peace for a few days, answer these questions:
Do you notice any physical changes, such as areas of pain, or tension?
Do you feel less stressed?
Do you feel like things flow easier for you?
Do you sleep better?
Do you feel like you have more energy during the day?
Do you have an overall sense of joy in your life?

You may want to journal any thoughts that come to you when you focus on reaching peace. Also, notice how you feel physically, mentally, and emotionally the days after you've practiced this for a few days.

Journal for Day 8

Day 9

I prepared to meditate with the wings and go to the crystal cave once again, yet I was always thinking the same thing each time. What will today's message or experience be? I never knew what to expect, and I always wondered. I laughed at myself for thinking these things.

So I reclined in my chair and placed my hand upon the points of the purple amethyst, and I allowed myself to drift away into the deep state of connection and meditation.

Your human life has been taken much too seriously. You have forgotten to have fun and to go with the flow. You have forgotten who you and how important your soul is to the greater whole of all of creation. You have forgotten why you need to experience the things you do.

Your physical form is automatic; you are made up of energy cells and molecules, and all of those things function automatically without effort. It is like your physical heart beating: it just beats on its own and knows what to do, yet when there is an obstruction of flow, the physical body experiences pain, disease, or illness in some way. It is the same when you allow things to happen for your existence on the earthly plane. If you let things flow in a fluid manner, then things will just happen automatically, the same as the heartbeat. It is the same as all of the inner functions of your body: your outer experiences will be the same if you just allow things to happen and go with the flow. When you stop the flow or run into a block, it is your own doing of blocking yourself by fear, or you ego telling you that you should not do something, or your refusal to relive something that you have done in the past. When you block yourself, or when you find resistance in something, that is when the energy stops and gets bottled up; it has nowhere to go, so it gets stagnant and drops off. When you allow it to flow, it continues the cycle of where it needs to go, and then it leads you where you need to get to easily and effortlessly. However, when the energy it is blocked and stagnant, it makes your efforts much more complicated and then creates stress, fear, and worry. Then of course there is what you call the domino effect. When positive energy flows, it flows, but when it is blocked, it stops and causes a pileup and a mess. When you try to control things, that is when the energy stops. When you try to force things, that is when the energy stops. That is when you experience negative reactions or resistance.

If you start to see everything is energy and vibration, it is much easier to understand this concept. Every component of life is energy and has a vibration, and if you realize that you are controlling and forcing something to happen, that will stop the flow of energy. This is a widespread issue. As you can imagine, there is so much energy stopped and bottled up in such areas that it is so dense and makes negative energy flourish. If you learn to allow the energy to flow and function as it is meant to, you will find harmony with all things, including yourself, all people, and all of creation—with all things associated with your life on earth.

We are giving you such deep information, and a lot of it will be hard to process all at once. We understand that. You must take small sections at a time and think about the things that we present to you and reflect upon them yourself. Challenge them if you will, because that is part of the learning process. We are here to help you on your path and to help you get where you need to go. We ask you to challenge what you have learned; we ask you to apply what you have learned and to let yourself experience what we have taught you. You have to unlearn all of the things that the earthly experience has taught you in all the many years that you have been here this time around. (When they say "this time around," that means the present lifetime we are currently experiencing. We have many lifetimes, past, present, and future, and we are currently experiencing "this time around.") *In doing so you have to restructure your thought process of how you think of things. Seeing everything as energy is a new way to think of things. This and these teachings will help you overall on your path to enlightenment. The more that you are able to absorb and apply in this lifetime, the more you will be helped in the many more lifetimes to come, and you will advance much more quickly.*

Our ultimate goal is for all souls to experience peace, harmony, unity, and divine love. So much learning has occurred overall, yet there is so much more to learn and so much more for you to experience. Allow yourself to experience, learn, and come to terms with the experiences you have had this time around. Oftentimes many find it difficult to let go of certain experiences they have had, and they block the healing from those experiences by refusing to revisit those memories or pain. You must heal them and move on. You must move past what has hurt you so that you can heal it and ultimately return to divine love. When you reach the state of inner peace you will be able to heal the past experiences that have caused you pain. The more that you practice these teachings, the more you will find yourself at inner peace and harmony, and you will find yourself in a more positive state of being overall. Furthermore, when you are in a more positive state of being, you will block negative energy flowing to you, and if negative energy does come to you, you will be able to handle such issues at a much quicker rate so as to realign yourself with all that is. (All that is, is the Creator, Source Energy, God). *That is an ultimate goal, to be in harmony with all that is. All that is means the Creator and creation, and you are part of that; you are made of the same energy. Everyone is part of all that is.*

I felt the pulsing in my fingers as the energy from the crystal went up my hand and my arm and surrounded my whole body. The information I received had been expressed with such passionate deliverance. I felt it was of great importance that these messages be shared with others. I felt that was all for today. I sat up on my granite bed for a moment, then stood and bowed my head, put my hands in prayer position, and exited backward out of the crystal cave.

Reflection on Day 9

Many of us are caught in the cycle of wanting to control everything. We want everything we wish for right now, and we want to control the outcome of everything we wish for. Sometimes when we try to force an outcome or direction and it is not aligned with our soul purpose, we run into blocks, but we keep pressing on, thinking that the particular direction we are trying to go in is the right direction.

Plus we are very impatient beings. We have forgotten to just be in the moment and appreciate the experience of getting where we need to go.

When we let things flow, it is a constant energy that comes and goes effortlessly. If we want something to occur, we should allow it to unfold and happen. Of course, we still need to put in effort and follow the guidance and direction that is presented to us, but if we allow things to occur and be part of that experience, then the flow is not interrupted.

Have you ever had that experience where you wanted something and kept trying to force it to happen, and you ended up beating your head against the wall because nothing was happening? That can cause a negative energy cycle such which may include emotions such as anger, doubt, frustration, panic, worry, fear or other negative emotions. The energy feels very rigid and that creates a block which contributes to the negative flow of energy within the cycle. I have experienced this a few times in my life. I was so frustrated that things were not working in my favor, because I was trying to control everything about the situation. Once I realized I was getting nowhere, I came to the conclusion that I was going about it all wrong, following the wrong direction, or just not meant to go down that path.

On the other hand, have you ever come across those people for whom everything seems to work out perfectly? They are in alignment with their true essence, and they allow things to flow to them. People that allow flow tend to be confident, happy, and possess an inner wisdom that everything will work out. Within my own experiences, when I have given up control, and allowed energy to flow, things just fall into place easily. It is like things just happen naturally and effortlessly.

All experiences are connected to our soul plan. Those experiences that resonate on a deep level and flow are aligned with our path. Those experiences that do not flow and get stopped in a blocked energy are not in alignment. That is not to say that what you want will not occur; perhaps you are just going about it the wrong way. This is also not to say that your wishes and desires are not important because they are not happening; that is not the case. Everything that you want is important because it is part of you. Again, maybe you are going about it the wrong way. You know the saying "Let go and let God"? When we give up control and let things flow, a good amount of the time the outcome is better than what we could have imagined.

Remember, with all that is presented here, just take little steps with what resonates with you. I see how this topic relates to yesterday's topic, because if you let energy flow and allow things to happen, you will be in a more peaceful state of being just because you will not have the harsh effects of trying to force something to happen. I believe it will all fall into place someday.

Action for Day 9

Think of a time when you held on too tightly to control or tried to force something to occur.
What was the outcome?
Was it difficult to get to the outcome?
Did you finally give in and go a different direction that was met with ease?
Do you think that allowing things to flow will help you in any way?
What do you see happening if you give up control and let things flow as they should?
Journal any thoughts and insights that come to you.

Journal for Day 9

Day 10

As I prepared myself for the day ten meditation, I sat in my recliner next to the big geode, placed my hand upon the points, sat back, closed my eyes, and accepted the purple ray. Let's see what today has to say, I thought.

The energy was so intense that I felt myself spinning and floating at the same time. I looked down upon myself within the crystal cave. I did not see myself enter this time, but I did see myself spinning right beside the granite bed. The energy today was very intense and powerful. Why is it so much more so today than other days? I wondered. I got my bearings and sat upon my granite bed, took a few deep breaths in and out, and then lay upon the bed, ready to accept whatever messages came through.

I saw myself lying there, and the intense energy was so very deeply healing, it reached down to the core of who I am. I felt all components of myself being healed as this purple ray penetrated my physical body and entered my soul. I experienced source energy surrounding me, and I became one and the same with it. I was almost dizzy because of this experience, and I had just begun. I was trying to process all that was happening, but I just needed to trust and let this unfold as it happened. I knew I was always in a safe space within this place, and I knew that I was surrounded by divine love and light, but it was so greatly intensified this time.

We want you to feel divine love so intensely that you do not forget it. Again, another importance that you must always remember is that you are surrounded by divine love; you are divine love. You are divine energy; you are created of source energy, and you have forgotten that you are a reflection of the Creator, of God himself. When you are faced with negative situations, try to react or respond in a loving manner. This practice will realign you with who you really are and your oneness with source energy, but it will also defuse the negative energy in your immediate area, as well as defuse the intensity of the negative situation.

Each and every one of you contributes to the whole when you are within the right alignment. You all have unique qualities to contribute to the whole when you are in the right alignment. What do we mean by a right alignment? That is when you are aligned with source energy and who you really are. It is your true soul essence. How do you get to that point, you might ask? You get to that point by continually connecting with who you really are and source energy through meditation, through walking in nature, and through appreciating all of the wonder and beauty that surrounds you each and every day. It is the simple things that matter: the scent of a flower, the soft breeze against your skin, the warmth of the sun, or a sip of cool water. All of these things are simple yet forgotten, but they are all beautiful components of the creation of which you are part.

You are connected to all energy, and all energy is connected to you. All things are energy. A rose is connected to you, and you are connected to a rose. By looking at it, appreciating it, and smelling its beautiful scent, you have appreciated it on a deeper level, and you gave it love by doing so. When you exchange energy in such a way, this type of experience provides a connection between you and the rose. It gave you joy and happiness for a moment, and at the same time you returned the joy and happiness to it. You both reap the rewards by expanding the positive life force, and you both continue to grow and flourish. You help each other during that moment of time just by appreciating and being grateful for its pure beauty and existence.

There are many variations in forms of energy upon the earth and what is around you that you cannot see. By connecting with the rose for just a moment, the energy that flows between you was very positive and pure. Water, fire, earth, and all the elements are very powerful, but you are powerful energy as well.

The more that come together with peaceful, loving thought, the more that Mother Earth will feel at peace. She responds to your thoughts. There is a collective group of negative energy in this period of time that continues to amplify more and more, and that is why the earth experiences continuous what you call natural disasters or natural powerful elemental negative energy in return. Mother Nature responds to how she feels overall from the vibration that you give her. Earthquakes, hurricanes, tsunamis, and all natural disasters are part of her feeling the collective vast negative energy around the world. Once more people start to focus on love and kindness with each other and respect for each other and Mother Earth, then you will see fewer such occurrences happening.

It is important to remember that all things are energy, and all energy has a frequency. Even the words you speak are energy. The thoughts you think are energy. If you say negative words, that sends out a negative vibration and frequency that continue on, because others will latch onto it and repeat it, which will cause fear and distress, and as the energy continues, it amplifies. Celebrate life, and continue to speak in positive words. Even in negative situations, continue to speak positive words and send out peace to block and defuse the negative vibrations from coming into your immediate aura or energy field. It is important to stop the negative-energy vibration from penetrating your being. The more who can accomplish this, the more positive energy will amplify and reduce the negative-energy vibrations and frequencies around the world. This is a confusing concept, and we will try to make it as simple as possible. All things are energy—that is one of the main components to remember. All things are energy, and it is up to you to reduce the negative-energy flow so that the earth and all creation can live in harmony once again.

That was the end of this discussion, and I felt depleted of my own energy because of the powerful and passionate deliverance of the message today. Right after their message was given, I felt the need to ground myself.

So I sat up on my granite rock and stood for a moment to get my balance, put my hands in prayer position, bowed my head, and gave thanks as I walked out backward of the crystal cave. I stood outside under the sun, and I accepted rejuvenation of energy it provided me.

Reflection on Day 10

As I reflected upon this discussion today, it seemed as though there was one thing that flowed to another, and it all happened so quickly that it was hard for me to keep track of what was happening. I came out of the meditation tired, and needed to ground myself physically. I also found myself questioning why we kept returning to similar topics. I knew it must be something of great importance if I was continually receiving similar messages. I thought it must mean we had not yet grasped the magnitude of how important this was.

I did feel such a powerful presence of divine love, yet at the same time, the power was so intense that it felt like they (the spirits) really wanted us to hear what was said. I also felt that we must try to remember that we are always surrounded by divine love, and just knowing that may help us remember to try to focus on our own positive words and thoughts.

I know it is a process for many of us, keeping our words and thoughts positive, but to me the passion that came through about the topic means that it is something that we as a collective group should really focus on and try to accomplish as much as possible. We are all connected with each other and with all other forms of life on earth. What we say and think is a reflection of what others feel and vice versa, so if we all begin to say and feel positive words and thoughts, then we will reflect that to others, and it will continue on and on. Even with animals and plants, we have this connection. If we respect all life, honor it, accept that we are all part of the whole, then we become realigned with the true essence of who we are and what we are made of.

Action for Day 10

Sit in a quiet place for a bit of time, and focus your attention on feeling the divine love that surrounds you. Visualize it, feel it, and see the beautiful energy that envelops your aura in a loving hug. Look at the colors that surround you, and notice how you feel when you let yourself feel this beautiful energy. Journal what messages come to you, what you saw, and how you felt.

Next, take a few moments to exchange energy with a piece of nature. Hold a flower, leaf, branch, or any other type of natural element, and spend some time sending it love and appreciating its beauty and existence. Hold it, look at it, touch it, and listen to what it tells you, and notice how you feel during and after this beautiful energy exchange. Journal any insights or messages that came to you during this experience.

Journal for Day 10

_____
_____
_____
_____
_____
_____
_____
_____
_____
_____
_____
_____
_____
_____
_____
_____
_____
_____
_____
_____
_____
_____
_____
_____
_____
_____
_____

Day 11

Before I started the meditation for day eleven, I took a moment to place my hands on one side of the wings and brush my fingertips over the large amethyst points. The energy was truly amazing. When I connect and share space with the energy that this geode emits, it feels like everything is right and as it should be. There is an intense power, but it is very positive and peaceful at the same time.

I once again placed my hand upon the points of amethyst, lay back in my lounge chair, and prepared myself for today's journey into the crystal cave. I noticed that today's energy was not as intense as yesterday's. It made me think before we even began that today's message would be lighter than yesterday's. I was immediately taken into the cave and in a meditative state, with visions and information surrounding me.

Then I saw myself walking through a wheat field with the sun on my face, blue sky, and the feeling of not a care in the world. I touched the wheat as I walked by and continued my exploration of this place. I looked around and saw beautiful fields and mountains in the distance. I heard the birds singing and saw butterflies floating about. Where was I going? Where was this, and what was it that we needed to know from it?

We keep discussing things that are most important from our point of view, the things that many people have forgotten when they came to earth. There are many things that you have forgotten, and what we touch on are some important things that you need to try to remember on a constant basis. It will take time to remember all the lessons that we have taught you, but the more that you focus on all of these lessons, the more they will start to fall into place. Then it will start to be automatic, and you will have a deep understanding and wisdom about why certain things occur and where your life existence fits within all of the things that happen.

Many of you have forgotten that you are on a path and have a purpose to fulfill for yourself and for helping others along the way. Everyone is on their own path, and yet you have made it so very complicated, and it does not need to be so. If you go back to basics and into simplicity, then it will be much easier. You have complicated things by involving fear, misunderstanding, and judgment, among other things. That is when things do get complicated, and you forget that you are on a path. Then you put yourself in survival or protection mode, which puts up the blocks. You have forgotten to just enjoy the experience of being here. You have forgotten to be in the very moment that you are in.

You allow your thoughts and your being to be consumed with worry over things that might not even occur. Your thoughts are consumed with things that have already happened that you might not have liked and wish had turned out differently. Your thoughts are over consumed; your mind is over consumed with things that do not truly matter. Let go of what has happened in the past. You need to heal from it, and you need to let it go. To do this you must forgive yourself and others who may have caused difficulty in the past. Send love and light to them and let it go. When you are consumed with worry over things that may or may not happen in the future, that is when fear develops, and that amplifies the negative energy into the atmosphere, which then in turn causes the law of attraction to bring you more of what you fear. Had you not been consumed with worry of the past or future, such occurrences might not have occurred in the first place. You must allow your thoughts to be consumed with peace and harmony and focus on a positive outcome for everything.

How do you do this? Reconnect with nature, and do so often. That is part of the vision we shared with you, to show you that reconnection to nature brings you to such a deep peace and harmony that all feels right in that moment of time. Part of your journey is to experience and to learn. When you reconnect with nature, you reconnect with source energy. This is probably the easiest way to reconnect with source energy, because nature is source energy just as you are. Spend time connecting with nature, clear your mind of all the worry that consumes you, and talk to the animals and trees. Touch the flowers, and listen to the breeze.

All components of nature already remember that they are created of source energy and part of source energy. All components of nature (except for the human) *do not question their existence but follow their paths with ease. A fruit tree will continue to bloom and produce its fruit and flow of energy without questioning its purpose for doing so. When you are truly focused on connecting with nature, then the worry, stress, and craziness in your mind will subside. That is when you truly reconnect with source energy.* (You can put yourself in a meditative state when connecting with nature by truly being in the moment with nature). *This is something we suggest you do often, and the more you do this, the more you will be able to remember where you have come from and who you are. You are source energy. That is what you need to remember. When you remember that you are source energy, that is when other things that are not important begin to fade away.*

When you are consistently realigned with source energy, that is when all things are right in your world, and all positive things will begin to occur. Of course, it is very difficult for the human form to remember that everything is source energy. The flowers are source energy; the sun is source energy; the breeze is source energy; the blades of grass are source energy. When you remember that everything is connected and everything is source energy, that will help you hold the infinite wisdom of all that is and assist you in all aspects of your physical journey.

So continue your journey, and walk in the fields or grass or by the ocean, and truly connect yourself with being in the moment as being part of and one with nature. Then you will be returned in that moment to a connection to source energy and all that is. This will dissolve the consumption of unnecessary worry. This will also give you a quiet mind to receive clarity about what direction you need to go or what decisions you need to make. This will ease the past pain that you have been holding onto for so long. The more that you can do this process, the faster the healing will begin, and the faster the guidance will continue to flow to you. As you connect with nature, talk to the blades of grass; talk to the grains of sand; talk to the leaves; talk to the breeze; and talk to the beetles on the ground. Get an understanding of what they know, and listen for the answers that they share. They are waiting to be heard!

I saw the vision of myself still in the field of wheat and the sun upon my face, and I closed my eyes, tilted my head toward the sun, and allowed the smile to appear on my face as I felt enveloped in divine love.

Then I was back in the cave, sitting upon the granite rock, still smiling at the wonderful experience, and I gave thanks and exited as I normally did. As I exited, I felt good and refreshed. I felt divine peace and love surrounding me. Today's experience was not as intense as the past few times, and I felt it was something that was much needed today at this point in our lessons and in our journey together.

Reflection on Day 11

When our thoughts and words are consumed with fear or negative emotion, we have detached ourselves from source energy. If we can recognize when such feelings occur, then we become aware of the importance of bringing ourselves out of that state to realign ourselves with source energy and who we really are.

By spending time in nature, we can focus on what is positive and pure in our immediate environment, and it will help ease the stress, worry, or fear that we were focused on prior to entering a space with nature. When we become one in the moment with nature and really appreciate and connect with nature, our thoughts and feelings start to become peaceful and back to harmony. We are able to breathe when we are in nature, because so many times we hold our breath when we are stressed or experience fear in some way. Some of us have had years of fear, worry, stress, anger, or other negative energy consume our lives. I was one of them. I lost many years to such energies. But once I was able to start letting go of the negative, the positive started flowing in immediately.

It can take time to undo years of emotional, mental, or physical stress, but stepping into nature, connecting with it and listening to it, can really make a positive impact and shift your energy very quickly. It is one of many tools that I use to keep myself on track so that I do not revert back to my old ways. Nature itself is so vast and unlimited that you have endless choices of how you want to spend time with it. The main point is to spend time in or with nature in some way, and you will begin to see things differently. You will begin to feel the negative drift away and the positive flow to you. Listen to what nature tells you. Your inner guidance understands that language.

Action for Day 11

Go out and spend time in nature. Go to the mountains, ocean, lake, stream, hiking trail, or anywhere else where you can spend some quiet time and connect with all that surrounds you in that place. Sit on a rock or in the sand. Feel the dirt, and enjoy the breeze. Notice how the sun feels as it warms your body. Touch a plant or a flower, and look at the details of it. Notice all the rich, deep colors and beautiful scents nature has provided for you. Appreciate the moment of spending time in such a place together in harmony. Notice how you feel when you are in that place.

Are you breathing better?

Is your heart rate normal?

Are any areas of tension forgotten?

What are you thinking?

Do you feel at peace?

Do any messages come through for you?

Journal all insights, visions, or other thoughts you may get during this process.

Journal for Day 11

Day 12

I began by settling in on my chair, closing my eyes, placing my hand upon the geode, and preparing myself to go into the crystal cave. I found it interesting that each day I did this, I could feel energy right away. Some days it was very powerful and intense, and other days it was a bit calmer. Today was quite peaceful. I felt like it aligned with the energy of the topic of the day. I guess we will see in a few moments, I thought, so here we go.

As I began going into the deep state of meditation, I felt this divine love and peace surrounding me. I saw myself inside the crystal cave, lying upon the granite rock, but I felt surrounded by divine love. The energy was so very loving, calm, and peaceful that it just felt right. It felt like everything was in place and in order and as it should be in this very moment of time.

We are pleased that you feel this love; it was our intention today that you focus on feeling divine love surrounding you. You get so caught up in your human life that you often forget that you are continuously surrounded by divine love. It is always there, no matter what you go through; divine love always surrounds you.

Sometimes when you go through difficult or challenging times, you forget the support of divine love and that it is there, and we are here to remind you today that it is always there, and that you are part of this divine love. You are loved, and this love surrounds you. For all those reading this, we are taking you on a journey. Wherever you might be, step outside with us, and let's go on this journey together. (It is best to do this exercise by reading through it and then doing it again later in your own time, so that you can get the benefit of seeing all the details in your own mind, because it will be your own unique experience). *Wherever you are, sit in a quiet place, and take some nice deep breaths in and out to clear your mind of any chatter. Then close your eyes, and let us take you on a journey. Visualize yourself walking into a very pleasant place. Do not worry about where you are walking; you are just walking. You feel good as you go to this place. You feel at peace. Maybe it is a place you are aware of, or maybe it is somewhere you are unfamiliar with. As you continue walking, you look at the sites and surrounding areas. You might see people or animals as you move along, and it is a very pleasant place. Pay attention to various sounds you hear, and notice the details of everything that surrounds you. Take it all in. You are safe in this place, because we are walking with you. We surround you in divine love, light, and protection, so just continue your journey as you walk along. Perhaps your journey may be walking on a street, a path, or an area with no designated walking space. It could be on a beach, or it could be in the mountains. Notice how vibrant the colors are. As you walk along, no matter where you might be, in the next few moments, you will come across a door. It is safe to go to the door and open it. When you are ready, open the door and see what is on the other side. This is your safe place. This is where you are free to be you. This is the place will you will experience divine love. Walk through the door, and look at your surroundings. Where are you now? Is it different from where you were before? Remember, you are surrounded in divine love. Find a place to sit and rest. It might be in the grass or on a chair or on a rock. Wherever that place is for you, sit and get comfortable. If you prefer, you can lie down. Get comfortable, and soak up the sun or the moonlight, whatever is surrounding you at that time. Feel yourself being enveloped and surrounded completely in divine love. You are loved unconditionally by your spirit guides and by the Creator, as well as by all those unseen who are here to assist you. It is our highest interest that you realize that you are loved and that you are love. We understand that you have gone through difficult times in the past, and there might be some challenging times in your future, but it is all lessons for you, and we are always here for you. We want you to know that we are always here for you. We are here for your support, and we are here to remind you that we love you. On the other side of the human life, the spirit side is complete divine love, and what we do is always for your best and highest good. So take a moment to feel this beautiful, radiant love surrounding you. It is possible you might feel some emotions come about, and that is okay, because that means that you are feeling and accepting the love that we are giving you. You are loved, and you are created of love. Feel the warmth. Feel the tingles. Feel the beautiful energy*

that surrounds you. You are worthy and beautiful in our eyes, and you are the perfect representation of you. Your shell of a body is just that; your soul is the most beautiful, radiant energy there is, and you need to remember that you are pure love. Feel this radiance surrounding you for a few moments longer, and know that you are special part of this experience on earth. You are a special part of creation, and you contribute greatly to this experience on this earth. You matter. You are special. You are loved, and you are love. Continue to feel this beautiful, peaceful, loving energy surrounding you, and anytime that you need to come back, you may do so, because this is your safe sacred space, and we encourage you to visit it often. As you feel this divine love surrounding you, notice if there are any animals or trees or flowers near you, or anything else that stands out. These are the symbols for you to remember that you are loved and connected and part of this greater experience of life. Anytime you see these same animals, flowers, or other things in your normal reality, you will be reminded that you are deeply loved and supported in all you do. Take one last moment to gather all the details, colors, and sounds that are in your sacred space before you return. Now it is time to go back through the door and walk back to where you came to return to reality once again. (Take a few deep breaths and open your eyes.)

We hope that this exercise has given you an experience of feeling truly loved, because you are. It is important to remember that you are loved and that you are part of creation that is all divine love. We want you to remember this always, because if you take this divine love with you and realize that you are divine love, then you will radiate that love out to others as well. You will affect others in a profound way, and they will not even realize how, because love is the most powerful energy of them all. If you are confident and know without a doubt that you are part of divine love from the Creator and are surrounded by divine love, you will radiate that divine love out to others, and it will expand and touch unlimited numbers of people in profound ways. Those who do not even understand what is happening will feel it, and it will make a difference to them and their life journey. There are so many lessons that we are sharing with you, but they are all rather simple if you think about it. By coming into the human form, you have forgotten of all the things that you knew to be true.

I stood up, bowed my head, gave thanks, and walked out of the crystal cave feeling surrounded by divine love.

Reflection on Day 12

This was a beautiful experience. I felt the great importance of remembering that we are so deeply loved by the Creator and the spirit guides. I think a lot of times we tend to forget this, or we are so consumed with life in general that we do not allow ourselves to feel that kind of love. It is such a deep love that I find it hard to describe. It is the most powerful feeling of love, knowing we have the complete and utter support and understanding for what we are experiencing. We should take time to recognize and to feel that love often. I do believe that if we feel that love, we reconnect with who we are, with our true authentic selves. When that happens, we radiate that energy to others, and yes, they will feel it. Others may not understand what has affected them, but they will sense the love coming from those who feel the divine love. That has the potential to impact thousands of people or more! Can you imagine what this life experience would be like if everyone felt love in some way or another? It would put this whole world back on course to where it once was.

Action for Day 12

Go back and reread the spirit message of day 12 to get an idea of how to allow yourself to go on your own journey to your sacred space. If it is easier, you can have someone read it to you, or you can record it yourself and listen to your recording. Find a quiet place, clear your mind, close your eyes, and take a few deep breaths in and out. Visualize yourself walking along until you find a door. Take in all the details as you walk. When you are ready, go through the door, and see what is on the other side. Find a place to sit or lie down in your sacred space and feel the divine love that surrounds you. Look at all the details and colors, and listen to what you hear. Pay attention to what surrounds you, because they are symbols to remind you that you are always surrounded by divine love. Feel the deep feeling of love. Then, when you are ready, return and journal your personal experience in detail.

Journal for Day 12

Day 13

I began my normal routine of getting settled in my chair, taking a few deep breaths, placing my hand on the geode, and allowing myself to drift off into the purple ray. "Dear spirit of the amethyst geodes," I said, "I am ready to receive and convey whatever information you wish to give us today."

We have given you a lot of information in a short amount of time. For some, that might be very difficult to absorb and try to practice on a daily basis. We want you to know that we are grateful that you are here to even listen to (read) what we have to say, because it is important that you know how we feel on the other side of physical life. Although we do not feel per se, it is important for you to know what we think is important for you to know. Try not to cause yourself any distress over trying to accomplish everything that we say right away, and give yourself some time to absorb all the things that we have told you. Reflect upon what you have learned, and see how you can apply it within your life. Take your time at it, and do not rush it. Let it happen. Let it unfold. If one thing that was conveyed here causes you to think about it, whatever that subject might be, then that is a step in the right direction. If you are thinking about it, then you are acting upon it in a positive way, even if you do not realize it as such.

Try not to take life so seriously. Try to remember to have fun and to take joy in the exploration of experience. Life on earth is about learning, experiencing, and finding out what your specific purpose is. Take yourself back to the childlike wonder of when you learned something new, how exciting it was, and how you felt like you had really accomplished something grand. Try to take yourself back to that time when you were unclouded with day-to-day pressures, activities, and obligations. Find yourself some time to just be with yourself. Be within the company of yourself, and reclaim who you are. Allow time to treat yourself kindly, and do what makes you happy. If you are in a happy state of mind and being, and you have happiness in your heart, that is a huge part of the battle that you have to overcome. Remember the little things that make you happy, and then find more of them.

Explore the wonder of all of creation. Simply your existence alone is such an amazing, beautiful ray of light. Find your light. Reclaim your light, and be your light. Let it shine for others to see. Take time to rest, treat yourself kindly, and love yourself. The rest will fall into place, but you need to take care of yourself on many levels, not only physically, but deeply spiritually at the soul level as well. Let yourself drift into daydreams. Let yourself sleep and dream. Let yourself flow wherever your mind takes you, and see where you end up. Trust and know that we are always with you. All of your spirit guides are always with you. You are always surrounded in peace, love, light, and protection.

There are so many things that being in the human experience has made you forget. We are here to remind you of those forgotten things. It is important to remember to be who you are in the moment and to reflect on your journey so you can appreciate your experience and yourself. You came into this life with a plan, and you are executing that plan. You are affected by other experiences and other occurrences, but you need to re-center yourself and remember who you really are to get back to your plan and path. Now go out and live your life filled with love—love for yourself and love for others.

I found it interesting today that for the first time, I had not seen myself inside the cave until I had finished receiving the message. I had immediately been taken into channeling without seeing myself go into that mode. I did see myself as I exited the cave, and I felt immersed in peace and love. It was a much more nurturing feel today, as each theme or topic seemed to resonate with the same vibration of what the crystal emitted.

Reflection on Day 13

Today's message seemed to be much more calm and loving. It was not such an overwhelming and powerful message as some days have been. Some days the masculine power comes through, but today it was much more of a nurturing, feminine, soothing energy, and it spoke to us in a firm yet mothering manner. We must have needed it at this point within the lessons.

It is a good reminder that our physicalness (humanness) typically does not allow us to do all that the spirits suggest immediately. It is difficult for us to drop everything and unlearn all that our society and culture have taught us over the years and then completely relearn what we are capable of, who we are, and what is important for us to focus on. That takes time. It is an adjustment. Like anything else, when we are learning, it takes time to think about what we have learned so we can begin to apply it on a day-to-day basis.

The process will be different for everyone, and everyone will begin at different places. We will make mistakes, and we will have times when we forget what is important, even if we practice it on a daily basis, but that is okay. It is part of the learning experience. Once we master something, we no longer need to learn it; it becomes second nature and automatic. I think consistency and practice are key components of the process. Just keep trying. With each step you take, remember they (the spirits) are always with us to support us, encourage us, protect us, and love us.

Another thing to remember is that we will never let those on the other side (spirit guides, the Creator, angels, etc.) down, regardless of what path we take or what mistakes we make. They will continue to love and support us regardless. They just want the best for us and to help see us through to where we ultimately need to go. At times certain emotions may arise when you begin to remember and apply what you learn, but that is part of the overall healing process of reclaiming who you are. Remember, as you do these things, you are always surrounded by universal love, light, and protection. Always.

Action for Day 13

Take some quiet time to reflect upon where you are in your life right now. Think about and answer these questions.

Are you happy with yourself?

Try to think back to a time when you planned on creating this existence for yourself and all the details of your life. Think about why you look the way you do, why you do certain things the way you do. Begin to appreciate your physical self for all that you are. Appreciate your soul for all the inner wisdom and love it holds. Remember how utterly special you are. Let yourself feel what that feels like.

Do you feel like you have learned on some level the reason why you are on the path that is your own?

Are you where you want to be?

Are you headed in the direction that makes you happy?

Are you looking for a new direction?

What would make you so happy that all other concerns would drift away?

Do you hear the deep voice within when it speaks to you? Do you listen to what it says?

Write in your journal all that comes to you, and then go take some time to experience the wonder of this beautiful earth. Take some time to do some things you enjoy.

Journal for Day 13

Day 14

I just realized that during these channeling sessions, I used my receptive hand. It made complete sense that I automatically placed my receiving hand on the geode to receive messages. It was easier to sit with these massive wings with my left hand touching them, so I found it very interesting that I was just guided to do that without even realizing it.

I also found it very interesting that there had been very intense energy for several days in a row, and now for the past few days, it had been much calmer energy. It seemed as though the energy was going in waves or cycles of its own—or maybe that was the best way we could relate to it. If it had been too intense each day, we might have been overwhelmed.

Today the energy felt very peaceful to begin with, but very quickly it started to get very intense, and I felt the vibration from my heart center all the way up my torso through my head.

I immediately saw myself in the crystal cave. I did not see myself walk into the cave, but I saw myself levitating or hovering above the granite bed. I hovered horizontally and spun clockwise like a wheel. I was not sure what this had to do with the discussion today, but I imagined I would find out soon enough.

For thousands of years, the human mind has been programmed for the limitations of the can'ts. In other words, they cannot do what you think or want to do. When you are in the soul space, you know better, because there you have an absolute knowledge that all things are possible and all things are obtainable. You know these things without a doubt and without question. Your soul knows everything it needs to know and everything you are capable of doing. The human mind and ego put the restrictions of the can'ts upon you. It is also the product of thousands of years of negative conditioning of human existence, and it is up to you to retrain your mind to break the barrier of the can'ts and turn it around to the cans.

The human experience was not always like this. Way before all of these limitations and blocks became prevalent, anything and everything was possible, and the human knew it. It was possible think of where you wanted to go and to teleport yourself there. You were able to focus on activities that made you happy, and you were able to live in harmony with one another and all of creation. Everyone lived harmony with Mother Earth and harvested her beautiful offerings with such deep gratitude and understanding of how everything worked. It was the breakdown of society and the corruption that followed that led to the blocks and restrictions that everyone began putting upon themselves. It was fear driven, and it has amplified over thousands of years so that you come into this life experience already with the thoughts of "I can't." There are some that do not have this issue—that is rare, but there are a few that are able to begin this lifetime and follow through with it always believing that they can achieve or obtain everything they want. It is time to start breaking the cycle and focusing on what you can do. You are capable of doing anything. You are capable of doing what makes you happy and being abundant at the same time. You have to reset your mind and belief system. In the human time frame, it takes time for this reset, because you have to break thousands of years of programming. So it does take time and effort on your part to stop believing the can'ts and start believing that you can achieve and become whatever it is that you want to and still lead a very happy, healthy existence upon this earthly plane during this lifetime.

We discuss being positive often, and we want you to have and maintain the positive vibrations as much as possible, because it allows the flow of wisdom and understanding on a much deeper level. Having the belief that you can means holding a positive vibration. It is an affirmation of something that you must put out there, mentally and verbally, that you can do whatever you want. Be sure to be specific with whatever it is that you want. Send it out there to the universe every day until you start believing it yourself. This is just another one of the processes that we suggest you apply to your daily life. If you continue to work with us and with these lessons, you will begin to see some positive changes happening in your life. You all have these gifts, or what some may call powers, within you to communicate with us on the other side, to teleport to another place, or to see things that will occur in the future or to regress and heal things from the past. You are all capable of all of these things and more. They are all within you, each of you, but these powers are dormant until you begin to realize they are within you and you are capable of using them. Yet again this is another thing that has been forgotten and lost from the spirit-to-earth transition and from the blocks of time. You all have these gifts within you, yet the degree varies from person to person. One person may be more apt to hear spirits, while another might be more apt to see spirits. However, all are capable of all gifts. You just need to understand and accept that you have them and then begin to relearn how to use them. This is part of your complex composition of who you are; it is part of you; it is part of everyone.

You are capable of doing many, many things. It is just that the human mind has been shut down and compressed from many years of society's dominance of what they want you to know and believe. Those that control these things are on their own learning path, and they will have to come to terms with these decisions they make within the next lifetimes in the future. It is their own learning progression, but certain things affect the greater culture and the greater human experience, so you have to learn to trust what is deep down inside you and let your true essence and energy come forward. If you believe deep down that something is not true, then it is not true. On the other hand, if you believe something to be the absolute truth deep down within yourself, then it is absolutely true.

This whole process is a relearning process; it is a relearning of who you really are. It is a relearning of what you are capable of and all of the components that make you who you are. It is a relearning of connection to the great source energy and that all creation, including yourself, is connected. It can be overwhelming to take in all of this at once, so take some time to reflect upon all of this information that you are given and that comes forward in your reflection time. The wisdom that comes forward will be very specific and very important to each individual who does this reflection time. We ask that you to take time to reflect on what we say and really think deep down inside and decide what it means to you. Then listen for what messages come from your soul. Your soul will respond, because your soul is infinite wisdom.

This was a very passionate conveyance of information today. When it was repeated in variation, it seemed to be very important that we understand and apply what was said. I felt my personal energy had been depleted from this session. I saw myself as I stopped floating and drifted down to sit upon the granite rock as I prepared my exit for the day. I gave my thanks and exited the crystal cave.

Reflection on Day 14

This was a powerfully intense session. When the words are spoken through me with such power, I can feel the intensity of the deliverance.

They say that when we enter the physical life, we come in with a clouded memory of what we know to be true. I believe that is because we are here to learn and experience, and if we came here already knowing what to expect, there would be no challenges to overcome, no lessons to learn, and nothing to really help us with the greater picture of our own personal path. So we come into the physical life with a clouded memory, but we also come into this life with the human history of many years of limiting beliefs, so oftentimes many people accept those as being the norm as we grow in our human body.

Once we break free of all limiting beliefs, that is the key to actual freedom. By doing so we will continue our path with no fear, and we will have the deep understanding of what we are truly capable of doing, regardless of what society or culture says. The things we thought we were restricted by are no longer there. We will start focusing on what is truly important: following our soul path and finding true happiness.

It is important to start to believing that we can do, become, achieve, or go anywhere we wish. It is important to release the self-doubt, that little voice in our minds that makes us question the truth. Follow the deepest part of your soul: that is the ultimate path. Listen to what your soul says, and go in that direction. Our soul will never send us somewhere we are not meant to be. It is time to trust and believe who we are and what we can do. We must break free of the limitations and regain our own confidence in all we do. Whatever we feel is important is important because it comes from the inner wisdom that we have silenced for so long. If we focus on what is important to us and listen to the guidance of our soul and spirit family, then we can move forward with the wisdom that created us. Then we can follow our true path.

Action for Day 14

Take some reflection time to think about how many self-limiting beliefs you hold right now. They can be related to money, health, career, family, relationships, or just about anything else. Next, make a list of things that are important to you but that you have put off for various reasons. Then write a specific affirmation to achieve or obtain the top thing on your list. Place the affirmation in places where you will see it often. Say it often and several times a day so you start to train your mind in believing you will receive or achieve this. Here are some examples you can start out with, but revise them to make them specific to your situation, or create your own that suit your needs.

I believe in myself.
I am capable of doing all I want to do.
I am filled with abundance in all aspects of my life.
I am creative, and I create my own beautiful life.
I can do it.
I will accomplish everything I set out to do.
I am a radiant being of light and completely healthy.
I walk in the light in all I do.
I trust my inner wisdom to provide guidance.

Write any thoughts that come to you in your journal.

Journal for Day 14

Day 15

I prepared myself for today's experience by settling in my chair and placing my hand upon the grand points of the amethyst. I began to feel the energy go through my fingers, into my hand and up my arm, and surround my body in this beautiful vibration of the crystal amethyst.

I saw myself stepping into the crystal cave and getting my bearings, because the lighting was typically a dark purple, although always very inviting and safe. It was illuminated by deep purple most of the time; each point radiated beautiful purple light, although when I looked into the cave, I could see quite clearly. I settled upon my granite rock and waited for today's message to come through.

You are all significant; you are all important; you are all worthy and deserving. If you have forgotten those things, you have forgotten your truth; you have forgotten who you truly are. Each and every soul is a big part of all of creation. Every soul is part of what created everything in existence on this earth—planets, solar systems, stars, and so on. Each soul has contributed to the creation of this vast universe. God the Creator, source energy, created every soul in the likeness of him—yes, that is true, and by doing so, you have become part of the Creator.

Look at it this way. In your human life, your parents had you, and you have attributes of your parents and grandparents, as well as similarities to your siblings. It is the same with God the Creator. The Creator created you, so you have attributes of the Creator. Because you have the divine Creator's essence within you, you can create the existence you wish. You have already created many components of what you experienced thus far in the earthly life, but it also contributes to your complete existence.

You each have a grand master existence plan, a plan that covers your whole entire existence, which is infinite and never ending. In the beginning each soul created its own existence plan, and within that plan was included each incarnation of where you might go to learn specific areas to contribute to that plan. During each transition time, which is the time in between incarnations, you revisit the plan and look at the whole grand plan and decide what else you need to accomplish to be at your highest level of love. In the beginning you knew this would take many thousands of incarnations and many thousands of years of learning and exploring. Of course, there is no time in the universe; you are the judge of time in the human form. But here on this side (spirit side), we have no time, so you cannot really compare how long it has taken you to get as far as you have come. This is a lot to try to understand, but you do not need to understand all of it right now.

Just know that you have a grand master plan, and every lifetime that you have incarnated in some way or some form somewhere, you have contributed to the learning of your master plan. Each time you incarnate you learn something new, whether you realize it or not. Sometimes you have very specific agendas that you want to accomplish, and given that the human has free will and no remembrance of having a plan, sometimes you do not accomplish what you set out to do. Sometimes you put in your plan some indications of what you want to happen, yet you do not act upon those indicators, because you do not know that those are part of the plan. Sometimes you do realize that the indications mean something and you do act upon those indications, and they can take you to something quite extraordinary. That can be part of your enlightenment process. You create this plan each time that you revisit the soul space when you are in transition. You decide what you want to accomplish in the next lifetime, and it is part of your grand master plan. It is discussed with your complete soul group, and if everybody is in agreement with each part, every other soul involved with your plan will contribute to your plan. At the same time, you will contribute to other souls' plans, and there are many layers of planning for many souls at one given time. Once all things are in place for all involved for your plan, and once you have your part in place for other souls, then it is time to reincarnate in hopes of achieving the goals you set for yourself. Again, remember that when you come to earth in physical form, you forget the plan and the lessons you hope to master. However, within the plan, certain occurrences are set forth that give you opportunities to make choices in order to learn the lessons you are hoping to master. Because of the clouded memory and human free will, there are times when the lessons will not be mastered because of fears, insecurities, or other reasons. Although there are times you might have to come back a few times to really gain a complete understanding of a certain lesson, once you gain understanding of a lesson, then you move forward from it. Of course, we have discussed components of this before, but it seems as though we need to revisit this topic in more detail. Your soul group supports you in any way that it can, and it is all done through divine love and understanding. It is all done for the best and highest good of your greater self. It is all done for you to accomplish and gain whatever knowledge you need to move you to the next level of your existence. There is no competition, and there is no urgency to try and beat somebody on the higher levels of enlightenment. In the soul space, everyone helps each other within your own soul group, and everyone accomplishes what they need to accomplish eventually.

You are all creators of your own reality; you have created all the situations that will contribute to your reality in this lifetime and the reality of everyone before and after this lifetime. You have the creation component from God source energy, and it is within you at all times. You have contributed to your own creation and your own existence, and you have contributed from that creation your existence as a community as a collective group of enlightened souls for the greater good. Once you learn that you are the creator of your own reality, you can create whatever you wish. If you are able create love and harmony within your own life, that will help others along their path—again, if they realize it or not. There are many instances we have discussed in which many people along their path might not realize that you affect them in profound ways, but it does help them along the way, and that is part of their plan and yours. Do you ever wonder why certain things happen in your lifetime? Maybe you are stuck in a cycle where things continue to happen over and over again, and you cannot seem to break the cycle. Maybe you have not learned the lesson of breaking that cycle and truly believing that you are capable of doing whatever you need or want to do. Perhaps there is something within that cycle that you have not learned or have not mastered yet. Possibly you need to be an example for somebody else. There are many instances and many things that could be related to whatever the learning experience is that you have set out for yourself. Or have you ever had those moments of epiphany when you look back at your life and understand why you needed to go through those difficult times the way you did? Maybe you see others in their own cycles or epiphanies, but it is up to them to understand why. You can assist, and in many cases you will be part of their plan, but it is important not to judge others for what they are going through. Everyone is on their own learning path; you can assist them and support them, but do not judge them, because they are on their own path, and they created their own reality just as you did. Some people might have some very deep lessons that they need to accomplish during this lifetime that you do not understand, and it is okay if you do not understand it. Just do not judge another person's soul path. That does not mean you have to accept what they are doing to be true and right from a human standpoint, but they are creating their own reality, and they have set out to put themselves in that position for a reason, and they must learn whatever lessons they have set out to learn. Do not judge another person's path. We repeat this because it is important to understand that each person is on their own path. You can send them peace, love, and light and can hope that they find their way and learn their lessons.

The beauty of the life experience on earth is that you set out to accomplish a plan that you are not aware of, and you have created your own reality, yet by learning this right now, you have the choice to create whatever it is that you wish from this point forward. You might not know what other lessons you need to master during this lifetime; that is typically a secret until you master them. However, you can create the reality that you wish from this moment forward, and doing so could very well be part of your master plan. Perhaps you were led here to help you with your master plan. You can create happiness within yourself. You can create peace. You can create abundance. It is up to you what you want to create, and when you create positive vibrations in any way, that again will radiate to others, and they will benefit from your creation because the positive vibrations that surround you will affect all those you come in contact with in a positive way.

We have a covered a lot today. This is a lot to take in, and it is a lot to think about. We challenge you to take some quiet time on your own and think about what you would create for yourself that would make you truly happy.

I saw myself sitting up from the granite bed, and I felt as though I was swirling with information that I personally had to process as well. I stood up and gave my thanks as I exited the crystal cave and returned to reality.

Reflection for Day 15

There was much information shared for this day. It can be overwhelming trying to keep it all straight. I think it is important to know where we come from so we can process and understand why we are here experiencing the things we do. We all experience different victories, and we all have challenging times in various degrees. Picture yourself in a large room with all the major players in your life. Can you see who has what part to play in helping you accomplish the goals of the lessons you need to learn? This may be difficult for some to visualize or even accept, so take it as it is meant for you. If this is too much right now, move on; if it intrigues you, continue your inner exploration of what you set out to do.

We are all created from source energy, so we all have that within us. If we have source energy within us, we should be able to create the reality we desire. When we find true happiness, our soul is in alignment with our physicalness, and all things are possible. When we are truly happy, that positive vibration affects all those around us in some way. It may just be the very vibration that another person needs to help them get through a struggle of their own. If more and more people held happiness within their hearts, they would be at peace, and the more people who are at peace and harmony, the more that will radiate to others, and the vibration will continue on and on.

We chose to be here. We chose to experience certain things to push us to the next level of our soul plan. The ultimate goal is to see all of creation with unconditional love, just as the Creator has. That is difficult to do, and that is why we come back to the physical form time and time again, to try to master small components to help us eventually get to that stage of existence of constant unconditional love.

Action for Day 15

As I stated in the channeling session, it would be a good idea to take some quiet time to think about what would make you truly happy. Really think about it, and take your time. Think about it on a deeper level.

What would make you happy? Journal all that comes to you.

Next, picture yourself in the soul space, discussing your plan with your soul group.

Do you recognize others in your group?

Do you see yourself as a significant part of someone else's plan? Then think about all of those who have come into your life who have either supported you or led you into a challenging situation.

What have you learned from those in either instance?

Could you see them as part of the grand master plan to push you to where you ultimately need to be?

Journal any thoughts you have on this lesson.

Journal for Day 15

Day 16

Today as I stepped into the purple-ray crystal cave, I felt the crystal vibration surrounding me. I saw the purple energy surrounding me, and it felt like waves and layers of energy, almost like a rippling effect radiating from the core of my being and back to me again. What an amazing feeling!

Today we want you to focus on that deep feeling at the core of your very being of who you are. Most of the feelings that you experience are on the surface. They are sudden feelings that occur when some instance triggers them. We want you to go deeper, as deep as you can, and feel with your whole heart, being, and soul.

Can you think of a time when you felt with your complete being that you absolutely knew something to be true? That is the point within yourself we want you to reach. So much beauty has just been almost passed over and unexperienced because you do not feel with your whole being. Take a flower, for instance—let's say a rose. Close your eyes for a moment, and visualize you are holding a rose. See yourself bringing the soft petals up to your nose, and let yourself experience the gift of the divine scent that it gives you. Take a moment to see yourself touching the soft petals, and let your whole being become one in that moment of feeling what it is like to experience that moment with the rose. You and that rose have become one in that moment of time. We want you to feel deeply, because that is when you expand your awareness to a much greater level. So if you feel a deep connection and feel deep emotions that come forward while you are holding and smelling the rose, you will expand your awareness about that rose, and you will expand your gratitude for that rose, and you will gain an understanding of its purpose for being there. You will expand your wisdom and your knowledge not only of the rose but of how to expand your awareness for everything.

The more you expand your awareness for everything, the more you will begin to understand on a deeper level why you are here and why you experience the things you do. Furthermore, you will begin to understand why others interact and experience things with you in the way that they occur. When you expand your awareness, you have a greater understanding of the universal laws, universal purpose, and love. You have a greater understanding of why there is life on earth and why you are part of it. Find the place deep within, and let yourself feel, truly feel. Of course, sometimes it can bring earthly emotions of joy, happiness, or sadness. Let the laughter or tears flow as they arise. You might also experience sensations such as tingling, muscle throbbing, waves of energy, energy traveling through certain limbs or around certain parts of your body, or perhaps a warmth or coolness on or around your body. Let yourself feel. Slow down. So much of the life experience during this point in time is spent concentrating on much that is really unnecessary. Slow down your breathing, and focus on your internal divine self. Focus on how you feel about things. Take the time to slow down and appreciate all things that have been created, and appreciate that you were part of those creations. Take the time to appreciate yourself for all the things you have been through and all the things you have learned.

You are divine because you are created of the divine. We repeat certain things because we feel that there is so much lack of understanding of importance, and we want to help you re-center yourselves on what is important for your journey. So many have put up blocks because they are afraid to feel. Yes, you have been hurt or are fearful or a combination of both, and you are uncertain of what will happen if you allow yourself to feel deeply. We understand that once you start allowing yourself to feel deeply and appreciate everything that you feel and touch and experience in some way, to feel it, truly feel it, you will have a deeper understanding of why things are the way they are or occur they way they do. You will have a deeper understanding of what will be coming next in your life. It is like you open a door to knowledge when you have a deeper awareness; you open the door to inner wisdom and universal knowledge. We suggest you start slowly, because it can be overwhelming if you have many emotional blocks surrounding. Allow yourself to feel one thing, such as a rose or other flower, or even spend a moment with one of your loved beloved pets. Spend some time really letting yourself feel and being in that moment with that particular thing that you choose.

The more you do this, the more you will heal and release the blocks that surround you and will start to trust yourself. That is another component of all of this: you have forgotten to trust yourself and what you know to be truth. So once you begin feeling deeply, you will begin to trust yourself, you will begin to release the blocks, and you will open your awareness to where you will have greater understanding of all that is.

I looked down upon myself in the cave during this meditation, and I saw this download of information coming to me. I knew that these things were very deep topics for the most part, but I thought that we would all be able to process them and take the knowledge that we had been given and open ourselves up to an even greater awareness than what we had before. I saw myself sitting up and placing my hands to my head as if I had received a great deal of information that I needed to process personally.

I stood up, put my hands in prayer position, bowed, and gave my thanks for the information of the day. When I removed my hand from the geode, the energy was pulsating, surrounding my whole being. It was very healing energy that was very powerful and very positive. I placed my hand above my heart center to receive the added energy within. I lay quietly in my chair just to keep absorbing the beautiful energy and information that had been given today.

Reflection on Day 16

I think most of us have put up blocks because we are afraid to feel. We have been hurt in the past, and we are afraid to feel that pain again. I can see the importance of allowing ourselves to truly feel things on a deeper level. I believe that by doing so, we will connect more closely with those things that cause us to feel, as well as connect to our inner selves and source energy. It is okay to feel. It is okay to allow ourselves to heal the emotional burdens we have carried so that we can feel with the depths of our soul. Part of the healing process can bring tears and or laughter, and it is okay to let those emotions flow. When we harness our emotions and hold them in, we cause our physical body to tense up, which causes pain or possibly illness. But when we release emotions and allow them to flow, that eases the tension, which releases the pain as well, both physical and emotional. I believe that if we connect to things on a deeper level, we will have a greater understanding of why those things are in our lives or how they can help our journey.

We are here to experience, and by experiencing we learn, and when we learn, we evolve. When we evolve, we become more closely aligned with source energy and who we really are. It is like a mature level of awareness.

Action for Day 16

Choose any object you want to connect deeply with for a moment. It can be a flower, a leaf, an animal, a rock, or any other natural object. I would stick with natural objects for this exercise, because they are created from source energy, and you can connect on a deeper level with natural objects. Sit quietly for a few moments with the object you've chosen. Close your eyes, and feel the object with your hands and fingers. Smell it, and experience the scent it gives you, if any. Appreciate all aspects of this object, and notice all the details of it with your eyes closed. Connect with it mentally, talk to it, and listen to what it has to say. It may very well have a message for you. Let yourself experience what it feels like to connect deeply with this object, and notice the emotions that you experience while doing so. When you are ready, open your eyes, notice how you feel overall, and journal your experience.

Journal for Day 16

Day 17

As I sat and prepared myself for day seventeen, I was in awe that I had spent that many days in meditation with this beautiful amethyst geode. So I settled into my chair, placed my hand upon the geode points, closed my eyes, took a few deep breaths, and drifted into the crystal cave once again. I immediately felt the energy going from my fingertips, through my hand, up my arm, and into my chest area. It was not long before the energy surrounded my whole body.

I saw myself step into the crystal cave, and I felt enveloped in love and comfort as I sat upon the granite rock. The energy today was very comforting, like a hug, like love was just surrounding this whole space. I settled in and prepared myself inside the cave for whatever we needed to receive today.

Today is more of a reassurance: we just want you to know that we are always here for you. When we speak of "we," it is not just us who are speaking to you but a greater sense of all spirit guides, including source energy, the Creator, and all of us who are on the other side of your reality. We never judge your decisions. You are on the earthly plane for experience and learning, and because you are in a cloud of what you have forgotten to be true, you are faced with many choices and decisions throughout your physical lifetime. Just know that we do not judge you. The choices you make are the choices you make, and there are things that you have to live with on this earthly plane and learn from one way or another. Do not feel heavy guilt over the things that you have done that you are not proud of. You should release that and let it go. It does not serve your highest good, and it holds you back in so many areas. We want you to know that we all love you unconditionally, without regard for anything that you have been through or chosen to do. We love you unconditionally.

We want you to know that you are special to each of us, you are part of us, and you are one of us; we are all one and the same. We want you to feel special; we want you to feel loved and comforted. Everything you experience is part of your plan, and we know what your plan is, but you don't particularly know it because you forgot it in coming to the earthly plane. When you experience challenging or difficult times, we want you to remember that you are always surrounded by divine love, and we will assist you if you ask for our help. If you can remember that, we will always be here for you, and you may call upon us for assistance with anything and everything. Call upon us for something very detailed or something very broad—anything that you need guidance on. We are here, and we want to help you.

It is in our highest interest to help you achieve what you set out to achieve and what is best for you. We want you to find what you are capable of, who you are, and what your purpose and path are. We want you to find the meaning behind the experiences and lessons that you need to learn from so you can move forward and advance in your own spiritual soul growth.

During this session, I saw myself sitting in a wheat field surrounded by nature, with the warmth of the sun upon me, and I held a single purple flower. I studied it and appreciated what it was and how it made me feel. Why was I seeing this particular scene right now? I knew that I had been here before; it was my sacred space. But why had I returned? (While I saw myself in this place, I had deep feeling of knowing that I was in the right place and everything was as it should be. I felt like I was more than content and at complete peace within and appreciation for all that was).

We give you this vision once again as a reminder for you to remember that you can always escape to your sacred place if you need to feel safe, loved, peaceful, calm, and where everything feels right. When you are experiencing a challenging or difficult time in your life, go into a quiet place, clear your mind, and go to your sacred space to return yourself to a place of peace. You can access it within your mind, but it is ingrained in your soul and is always there. It is an escape from things that cause you stress. Go to this place to clear your mind and find peace so you can react to the stressful situation in a clear manner rather than proceed with emotions that do not serve you. When you go to the safe sacred place, you can also find spirit guidance. It can be easier to talk to us while you are there, and it is easier to hear us as well. While you are in that space, you can learn and grow and understand so much on a deeper level.

"Please remind us, how do we achieve this?"

It is different for everyone, but we suggest you visit your sacred space quite often by meditation, daydreaming, dreaming, or even just quiet time. To enter this place in meditation, focus your intention on entering your sacred space, and see where it takes you. You will be able to revisit that specific place anytime you choose to. If you want to try daydreaming or quiet time, close your eyes for a moment in a quiet place, and let your mind drift to your sacred safe place. You will know when you reach your destination because it will feel familiar to you. You can also achieve this during your dream state; however, you would need to set your intention before you fall asleep, if that is when you would like to visit your sacred space. During the dream time, you might remember it, you might not. So to begin, you might want to try one of the other methods first. You will better remember your sacred space during and after meditation, daydreaming, or quiet time.

I felt the energy become more intense as it surrounded me, but it felt good, and I felt the deep, rich purple color penetrating my very soul. As I absorbed it through my fingers, it traveled throughout my body. I sat up and prepared myself to exit the cave for the day. I gave thanks, stood, and exited the cave. I removed my hand from the geode and felt my body vibrating with the purple ray. I felt good. I felt loved and supported. I felt like I was understood, and sometimes we need a validation that spirit understands us. I felt confident, and like everything was as it should be in this moment in time.

It was a beautiful experience. I wish that you could experience what I experienced when I did these channeling sessions. I wish that you could feel the vibration of the crystal. I wish that you could really feel how I felt and what I experienced during the whole session. I know my words come through, but it is not quite the same as experiencing it firsthand. Maybe you should hold an amethyst crystal as you read the following pages. Just a thought.

Reflection on Day 17

This was an experience of love. It was a deep unconditional love for my whole being, and I send it to you. You are loved unconditionally. We tend to forget that we are so deeply loved from the other side of physical life. When we remember that loved, we feel supported and connected. It is like any support system: when you feel that you can communicate freely and listen freely, the answers come easily. It is the same as communicating with the spirit world. When we talk and listen, the answers come easily.

I found it interesting that we discussed the sacred safe place again. It must be important if we revisited that topic. If we have to travel to our sacred space to find and hear those answers, then it is worth it. It is quick and easy to do, and I suggest you do so as much as possible. Find your sacred space. It is a unique place for all of us, but we all tap into the same universal love and guidance by going there. It is a special place that no one can take away from you. It is always there and accessible. When you go to your sacred space, that is when transformation happens. That is when the physical issues fade away and we realize that only love matters. When we feel that love, we feel deep inner peace and wisdom as well. When we are put into a challenging or stressful situation, that is the time to go into that sacred space to find inner peace and guidance. It is an easy way to connect to spirit and our true selves. Just by finding that deep inner peace and clearing the distressed mind, we can begin to re-evaluate the situation that caused stress in the first place, but with a calmer mind and clarity about what we should do. The key is to remember this when challenging times arise.

Action for Day 17

Take a moment to find a quiet time to enter your sacred safe space. Close your eyes, and take a few deep breaths. Let your mind wander and take you to your safe sacred place. When you enter, notice all of the details of the space. Notice the sounds, the deep, rich colors, and the scents. Notice how at peace you feel and how good it feels to be in this space. Find a place to sit or lie down in your sacred space, and ask for guidance with a specific issue you may be facing. Then listen to what kind of answers come. The answers may come in the form of colors, certain objects, voices, or something else. Remember, this is your safe sacred space, and you are safe here. Everything that comes to you during this time is for you, your peace of mind and body, and guidance. Feel the divine love that surrounds you. You can also reread chapter 12 to get the prompts given from the spirit to find your sacred space. When you are ready to leave your sacred space, open your eyes, and journal your experience.

The more you practice going to your sacred space, the easier it will be for you to return to it the next time.

Journal for Day 17

Day 18

As I prepared myself for today's session, I placed my hand upon the points of the geode and felt myself very relaxed and calm. I let the gentle vibration enter my hand, and it went up my arm, through my body, and touched my soul.

I settled into some nice calm breathing and let myself drift away as I entered the crystal cave once again. I saw myself in the center of the room, lying upon the granite rock, awaiting the day's message.

You have made your life so very complicated. You have created this way of life that leads you to feel like you need more than you do. Everything that you need is within you; it is deep inside, and you have forgotten how to tap into that. You have every answer to every question within you. All of these things that you feel you need complicate your life, and all of these energies that surround you daily complicate your life. It is part of the experience. It is also part of the experience to learn to let go of the things that make you not understand who you really are. You worry about things that are not necessary. Look down deep inside within you, find who you really are, and you will have the answers to all of your questions. When you find your place of peace and happiness within your heart, then you can be reassured that you are on your true path. Regardless of what your mind or ego might say, follow what makes you happy, because that is your path; that is an indication of your soul plan. When you feel that deep happiness and peace within, then you know you are going in the right direction. At that point, worry and concern will fade away, and trust will begin to encompass you. That is when you learn that everything is as it should be and everything is right for you.

When you start to uncover the complications of all the clutter and things that do not matter, and you peel away those layers to bring you to this place of understanding what makes you happy and peaceful, then you find what really matters. Then you realize what is truly important. That is when you no longer compare yourself to others; you accept who you are, and you find certainty of your direction. Self-discovery is an enlightening process, and there is so much for you to experience when you are in the self-discovery mode. You will come to understanding so much more than you can ever imagine. So much will start to make sense to you, and so much wisdom and understanding will present itself to you. You will realize what is truly important for you in this lifetime experience. If you waste your time doing things that do not make you happy, then you will continue that cycle, perhaps even into the next lifetime.

We want you to advance to the next level—that is why we are here to help you. We are here to help you understand what you are capable of and what you need to do to get to the next level of your own journey. So if you feel you cannot get out of something that you are stuck, in that is a negative cycle, and you will have to break free of that. It is very important to break free of a negative cycle and do what truly makes you happy. Then you will see the shift in energy occur, and you will have the enlightenment process open to you once again. You will be following your true soul path with a much greater understanding, and you will know where you need to go from there. You will have absolute knowing without question and will trust yourself and the universe, knowing that you are all one and the same.

How do you do this? Start by doing things that make you happy, whatever that might be. Find things that make you feel such a deep peace and happiness within that you are overjoyed to live each day you have left. It is as simple as that. Do not give yourself an excuse that you cannot find this happiness. No more excuses. It is time to move on from the negative cycle into happiness and peace.

I sat up, gave thanks, stood, and exited the crystal cave.

Reflection on Day 18

As I reflect on this meditation, I feel that the message overall was very strong and delivered straightforwardly. It is as if we are being told, "No more messing around. Get busy doing what makes you happy. There is no time to waste." We all have obligations, responsibilities, or people to take care of and schedules to keep, but within our busy day, we can take a few moments to do what makes us happy. It does not have to be complicated, and do not over think it.

We are so consumed with schedules and obligations and appointments and things we feel we have to accomplish and that we think are important, but truly finding our own happiness should be should be a priority. We are never taught that our own personal happiness is a priority in life. Well, it is time to start thinking that way. It is time to shift the energy in that direction. When we are happy, beautiful things start happening. Worry fades away. Stress fades away. Tension is released. When we are truly happy, life seems so sweet.

Start off simple, and expand from there. What is a simple thing that makes you happy? For me it is spending quiet time with my dogs, outside, with the sun on my face. Start with something small, and build upon it. Paint a picture, mold some clay, spend some time with those who make you feel special, play the piano and get lost in the music, go for a swim or a walk on the beach. The possibilities are endless, and the things that makes us happy are as unique as we are. Find some time to do something for yourself, something that brings you such happiness and peace that you recognize it truly makes you happy.

The more you can build upon it, the more you will find positive, beautiful energy starting to dissolve any complications you have created for yourself. Then you will also start to discover where your path needs to lead you, and you will see inspiration and creativity begin to flourish. I have found that when I am in the "truly happy" vibration, everything seems to work better, and wonderful things flow to me effortlessly. Doors that used to be hidden and closed are now open, and exciting new opportunities present themselves.

When we are in a state of happiness, life itself seems to be peaceful overall, and things that used to worry or stress us no longer matter. It is worth it. Give it a try, and see the positive changes that are right in front of you, waiting to be discovered.

Activity for Day 18

Take a few minutes today to write a list of what makes you happy. Get your journal, take a few deep breaths, and just let the words flow onto the paper. List as many things as come to you—anything and everything that makes you happy. Then look over your list, and pick one or two things to start with. If you have a busy schedule, schedule a time to do your happy activity. If you have a flexible schedule, just go out and spend some time doing your activities. Try to do this each day, and expand the time on some days if you can. If you do a five-minute activity today, try to do a twenty-minute activity tomorrow. Switch up the activities as well. You can do different things each day; it does not have to be the same thing every day. The main goal is to focus on things that make you happy and bring you to a state of peacefulness. Write any other thoughts that come to you in your journal. After a week or two of doing small things that make you happy, notice if you see a shift in your energy.

How do you feel overall?

Are you less stressed or worried?

Are you sleeping better?

Do you feel better about yourself?

Add the answers to these questions in your journal as well.

Journal for Day 18

Day 19

Today, right before I settled in to start the meditation to enter the crystal cave, I was surrounded by angels, and I heard their song. It was so very soothing and calm and comforting.

I placed my hand upon the points of the geode, closed my eyes, and settled into my chair to accept whatever message would be given today. I felt very positive, radiant energy today. All days have positive energy, but the energy is not always the same. This one was more of a glowing feel, warm and comforting.

I was immediately taken into the cave, and information already surrounded this place. There was so much information to be extracted from this beautiful amethyst. I almost felt dizzy upon entering this time, but I moved forward and saw myself walking slowly and lying down on the granite rock.

Life on earth is a special experience, and that is why many choose to experience their lessons upon the earthly plane. Life on earth provides many opportunities to explore and learn through each experience in a very quick manner. You feel as though your time is short or long, and you govern yourselves with time, but you learn so much in a very short duration within your life on earth. That is why it is so appealing for many to come here and learn lessons quickly. You might feel like you are stuck in a rut and that things never change. However, your time on earth is just a speck of dust in the grand scheme of it all. It is a tiny bit of what your existence is. Sometimes you might feel like you are stuck and not going anywhere, yet it is really insignificant compared to the whole big picture. As we were saying, many souls prefer to come to earth because it offers many opportunities for a learning experience in a short amount of time. The more quickly you learn and the more you learn, the more you graduate to ascension.

There are many other life forms and planets that you have the choice to experience, and many of you have. They are as infinite as everything else. Every soul has the opportunity to decide where their learning best suits them at the particular point in their journey. Earth is a very fast-paced learning experience, but other planets are not so accelerated, and it takes a bit longer to achieve the goals that you set out to achieve. Some other areas of life existence are more of an inner exploration in which you go to deeply focus on your inner being and your soul work and soul exploration. What you call aliens are just different souls in a different form that suits the life structure of where they currently live to learn their own lessons. You all come into your life forms as a fogged memory of sorts so that you have more opportunity to really learn what you have to learn. You come to earth and are greatly influenced by all of your surroundings, physical birth parents, culture, and community, and you learn in the structured setting, which just continues with the social settings of learning and the greater influences of the whole of earth. With everything that is happening around the earth, the more you grow, the more you are influenced by everything that surrounds you, and you forget to use all the wisdom that you hold within you.

We speak to you often about how you have forgotten so much, and we are here to remind you in a loving manner that we want you to try to remember where you really came from and what is really important and to follow your true heart and your true path. This experience here on earth is very quick, so make the most of it, and learn what you can. Do what you can to make yourself happy and to follow your path. Make the changes that you feel are necessary to help you accomplish your goals in a positive manner. Generations on earth have made things so very complicated, and you are so vastly influenced by so much.

Everything you need is within yourself, and it is always within you. You just have to tap into it and retrieve it, and we are here anytime you need guidance or assistance. Anytime you wish to tap into that deep inner wisdom, ask us to help you and we will. So we want you to remember that you have everything within you that you need. You have forgotten to trust yourself. You have forgotten to really believe that what you feel to be truth is true. It is all there in front of you. Take some time to revisit yourself and your beliefs, how you feel about where you have come from and where you are trying to go, and what you want to do to change it to make things right for yourself.

Everyone must focus on themselves. Yes, you need to help each other along the way, and that is important. However, you need to prioritize yourself as the number one person in your life. If you continue to help everybody else instead of yourself, you will get lost. You are here for your own experience, and you chose this experience, so make the most of your short time here, and make it the best possible time that you can. Enjoy it. There is so much here to enjoy. The earthly plane is one of the most beautiful places to experience and learn within the universe, so enjoy the rest of the time that you have here, and make the positive changes that allow you to follow your path.

I felt a heavy vibration as this message came through; my hand throbbed with energy from the geode, and I responded, "This is a lot of information, and many of us will have to really reflect upon this to absorb it properly." I gave my thanks as I exited the crystal cave once again. I found it interesting that the energy had started out calm and warm but then got very intense quickly.

Reflection on Day 19

I think that when we look at our whole life, we have to pull apart all of the main things that have happened to us and all the experiences we have had, the good and bad, and consider what we have learned from those experiences as individuals and as a collective whole. Then we must decide what it all means. We really have to do some deep thinking about what all this means to us and where we go from here.

We heard a good reminder today that life is very short here on earth, and we should experience all that we can in the best possible way with the time we have left. Make the most of all the experiences that we have before us, and go out and try things we have always wanted to try. Go out and experience this beautiful earth and all that it provides.

Let's try to reclaim who we are and make positive decisions, and not let outside influences be our driving factor. We need to trust our inner guidance and trust the universal guidance for all that we do. We have our own GPS system that we have forgotten to use. It is time to start trusting who we are and what we are capable of, really paying attention to what is important to us, and honoring what that is. By honoring ourselves, we can bypass being negatively influenced by others and negative situations. We have everything we need within us. Let's start to use it.

Action for Day 19

Take a few moments to ponder the following questions. You may be surprised at your answers and the insight that follow.
Are you curious about other planets and galaxies?
Do you ever feel like you have been to other planets, galaxies, or in outer space?
Do you ever feel like earth is a temporary place where you reside?
Do you ever wonder if there are other life forms elsewhere in the universe?
Do you feel like deep down inside, you have all the answers to all your questions?
Do you feel like life on earth is a short period of time?
Do you feel you can ask spirit to help you when you need it?
Do you feel you can trust your inner guidance?
Do you think you can enjoy yourself here on earth?
Journal the answers and insights that come to you.

Journal for Day 19

Day 20

As I sat and prepared myself for today's session, I felt very relaxed, and I placed my fingers upon the points of the geode. The energy felt very relaxed today. I find it very interesting that each day, the energy correlated with the message that was conveyed. That being said, I felt like today's message would be more relaxed or calm, but again, I never knew what to expect, so I would see what happened.

I closed my eyes, took a few deep breaths, and felt the energy radiating up my arm, but this time in a very subtle way. I let myself drift as I entered the crystal cave. I stepped inside, got my bearings as I accepted the purple ray of light, and settled on the granite rock in the center of the room.

Next, I saw myself levitating horizontally over the granite rock. I felt like I was being transported out into space, and then I saw myself being taken out into the depths of the great blue-black wonder of the universe. This is not like a teleportation journey, which goes by very quickly; this one seems to be much calmer and easier, like a relaxing trip. I saw the neighboring planets as we passed by, and I looked at their beauty and richness of color. I passed many other stars, planets, meteorites, asteroids, the moon, and the sun. The sun was a brilliant golden-orange molten liquid, and I felt its powerful energy. The moon was so very quiet and calming. The universe burst with colors, so many it was like a splash of different colors everywhere I looked. The space was filled with brilliant shades of yellow, orange, magenta, green, and blue intermingling with each other. When we look up at the night sky, we see black, but it is actually a deep violet blue. The energy in space is very energetic, to say the least. There was so much vibration that it almost overwhelmed me as I took it all in. We went farther out into the universe and galaxies, and I saw the earth as a disc in the distance. She was so very beautiful with her shades of blue, green, and white.

We want you to see some components of the earth from a distance today. We take you here to discuss looking at things from a distance overall. The earth comprises many good and wonderful things, and many good and wonderful things are happening continuously. Many times, several people are caught up in the negative energies that surround them or in things that may occur that cause negative emotions or energies to arise. But overall the earth is actually very stable and healthy. By looking at her from a distance, you can tell the pockets that are filled with negative energies. Those radiate red, while the rest radiate a calm blue-green hue. The areas consumed with war, hate, and greed are the ones that have red saturation, but overall the earth is very beautiful; there is more green-blue hue than red. Those who allow themselves to be consumed with things such as war, hate, and greed escalate the energy so it consumes many more, but it is not as widespread as you would think. It is there, and it is a problem. That is why we want you to concentrate on making a difference with your thoughts and your actions by radiating positive energy.

Every single positive word spoken or thought, every positive action, such as kindness, smiles, or laughter, will reduce the negative energies in those pockets that are consumed with negative energies.

If you experience a negative vibration or negative energy in some such way, then take a moment to defuse it and convert it into positive energy. Even if you have to take some quiet time and do some breathing, close your eyes and think of something that is very beautiful and pleasing to your mind. Perhaps it is a beautiful sunset or a walk on the beach. Maybe it is a baby animal that is so very innocent and pure, or it is a child's laughter. All of these things can start the process of reducing the negative experience you had and bring you back into the positive, which will then reduce the negative vibration in those pockets where it is heaviest.

Each time you can transform a negative vibration into a positive, it will make a difference not only with how you feel but with the greater whole as well. The more that you remain positive, the more profound effect it will have on the negative areas. Say for instance something has angered you. Perhaps somebody said something that you did not agree with, and you feel anger toward that person or the situation. Well, that is more about them than about you, because that is not who you are. If you accept what was said, then you become part of that vibration; if you reject it and return to who you really are, then you remain in the positive state. If you find yourself becoming angry over something, take a few deep breaths and really think about whether the anger is worth the side effects. Does what was said resonate with you? Is what was said truth? If you answer no, then you need to defuse the anger, close it off, let it go, and return yourself to the positive state of being. Commonly, when you act in anger, you are reacting to somebody else's action, but it is their issue to deal with; you are simply responding to their vibration. If you respond in a negative way, the negative vibration will continue and could possibly consume you for a period of time. If you respond in a positive way, then you cut the negative vibration off from yourself, and you recover much faster. If you find yourself in a negative situation where there is a great deal of heavy energy for whatever reason, send your requests out to your spirit guides to surround you in pure, positive, protective light, and then send blessings to yourself and each and every person within the area, and focus on positive, loving, kind thoughts. The more that you can concentrate on being positive, the better overall effects it will have for the earth and all its inhabitants. For each person who does this, and the more often they do this, the overall vibration of harmony will occur much more quickly.

As I looked from the distance in space down to Mother Earth, I felt it was nice to have a perspective to see these pockets of negative energies and to understand that they really were not as widespread as it felt like sometimes.

Yes, we want you to realize that you are important and that all of your actions, words, and thoughts are a contribution in some way. The more you keep positive, the more positivity will radiate to the rest that need it so desperately.

"I know my time here in space is limited, and I thank you for bringing me here," I said. "It is more beautiful than I ever imagined. I am so very grateful to be able to see this, and I wish my readers could see what I see as I experience this beautiful, awe-inspiring moment."

I was then taken back to the cave. I stood, bowed my head, and gave thanks as I exited the crystal cave once again. As I exited, I looked at the sun with great appreciation. I gave thanks to the sun and the moon, and I gave thanks to all of creation that surrounds Mother Earth, because there's so much more out there than we can even comprehend, and it is also loving and supportive.

Reflection on Day 20

There are so many people who are filled with pureness of heart and who want to do good, and even if they are not aware of it or do not understand it, it still helps overall. I understand that many of us are on this spiritual path, and our understanding is coming into a much greater awareness than ever before. So it makes sense to me that all of our positive actions and deeds toward one another do contribute to the greater whole of all of earth and those who reside here.

If we experience a challenging or difficult situation that puts us in a negative frame of mind, we have a choice to make. We can remain in the negative, or we can stop the negative flow and start thinking positively. Either way, whatever vibration we send out continues to others. We do make a difference, and I feel it is important for each and every person to realize that we do make a difference by each and every positive thought, word, and action. It might not feel like it, and you might not see it, but it does contribute to the greater whole of all of humanity.

Action for Day 20

Take some quiet time to think about the following questions.
Do you feel that your thoughts, words, or actions affect others?
Do you think it makes a difference to the greater whole if you think positively?
Do you think a collective group of people thinking positive thoughts really makes a difference for the overall vibration of life on earth?
Journal the answers and insights that come to you.

Journal for Day 20

Day 21

As I prepared for day twenty-one, I placed my fingers upon the tips of the amethyst geode, reclined and got comfortable in my chair, and let myself drift into the purple-ray cave once again. I felt the energy begin to enter my hand, go up my arm, and surround me in this beautiful vibration, this amazingly beautiful amethyst vibration.

I saw myself in the crystal cave, and I appreciated its simple yet divine beauty. I settled upon the granite rock in the center of the cave and awaited the message for the day.

Yes, this is the end of our journey at this time, but we will have other profound messages for you in the future. We want to thank you for taking the time to read what we have said. We ask you to think about what we have said and to attempt to put in practice what we have suggested. We understand that we have given you much to think about, and it can take some time to absorb all of the things that we have discussed here. We want you to know that we love you and that you are surrounded and filled with divine love, just as your true essence is divine love and everything that we do is through divine love. We want what is best for your journey, for your highest and greatest good, and for your learning experience and your expansion.

We also want you to know that you are special and capable and deeply loved on such a level that you cannot even imagine what it feels like, but we want to tell you anyway. All the universe loves you. The Creator, gods, goddesses, angels, and all other guides love you deeply. This is what it is on the other side: complete and utter divine love. So our messages to you are delivered with love. We hope that you receive these messages with love and understanding and acceptance. Always remember that you are a being created by love, which makes you love. We would like to see you take these messages and practice what you can, develop what you can, and try to understand something from these words that you read. Try to understand yourself at a deeper level than you did before you began reading these words. We hope that you find that inner wisdom that will guide and lead you for the rest of your days on earth.

Take these words and go with peace, love, and understanding, and you will reconnect yourself with all that is and all that you are, because it is all the same. Also remember that you make a difference not only for yourself and your journey, but by your actions and your wisdom, you will be able to affect others in a glorious, positive way. Your energy will radiate to others, and it will make a difference in the Harmony Movement. You will begin to see many changes within life on earth. You will begin to see many changes within yourself and how others react to you in all that you do. You will make a difference. You might not see it all of the time, but your positive actions will make a difference to others and to the greater whole of all of the community of earth. Take some time to reflect upon all of these lessons. See how they fit into your personal life and how you might be able to use or expand upon some of these teachings. We have spoken about energy many times. If you visualize beautiful energy in the most radiant colors you can ever imagine, you will understand what the universe comprises—beautiful, radiant, loving energy that is filled with color, light, and life. You are very special part of that.

I felt in awe as I saw these radiant colors surrounding us, all of us— brilliant whites, yellows, greens, blues, purples, and pinks, all intertwining to create this beautiful ray of colorful energy that enveloped all of us in its love and understanding. It was the most radiant, beautiful sight, color stretching as far as I could see.

"Thank you so very much for this time and this information that you have shared with us," I said. "I myself will continue to move forward and work upon the teachings that you have given, and I know that these words will help somebody besides myself along the way. Thank you for coming through and giving us this message."

I prepared myself to exit the cave. I bowed my head and gave thanks one last time as I stepped out of the cave and into the brilliant sunlight. I felt refreshed, rejuvenated, and as if there was new hope for all of humanity. I felt confident that love will thrive. As I released my hand from the geode, I felt the beautiful ray of radiant purple light filling my whole being, surrounding me in love.

Reflection on Day 21

Love is what it is all about. If we can hold onto the feeling of love for all things, then we have mastered the lesson. Unconditional love: that is what the other side is, the spirit world, and that is what they feel for us. What a beautiful feeling it is to know that we are loved so deeply. We will be continuously supported throughout our lives here and in all that we do, regardless if we make mistakes or take a wrong turn. We will be continuously supported and loved from the spirit world. This was a beautiful journey, and I cannot say this is the end. I believe this is just the beginning.

Action for Day 21

Take some quiet time to ponder the following questions.
Do you feel any differently about your life now than when you started this book?
Do you see things more clearly?
Do you feel different?
Are you more at peace?
Do you have a sense of what you can do that can help you with your own personal journey?
Journal everything that comes to you in thinking about this reading experience.

Journal for Day 21

Final Thoughts

First off, I want to thank you for joining us through this experience. I hope that you experienced beautiful energy, as well as some helpful information that you can apply to your own life. The energy from these sessions was beyond beautiful and amazing. I hope that you felt the divine energy coming through each day. The spirits made us aware of many important topics. It can be difficult and overwhelming to remember to do all of the things suggested on a daily basis, so just start where you can, and continue from there. Each day you can build upon the previous day for greater understanding to help you move forward within your own personal learning. All of the insights and aha moments that follow the day's lessons are meant for you, so use the wisdom that comes to you for your own self-exploration. I believe each person who was guided to this book was meant to read what was said for their own personal journey.

As an overall message from the spirit of the crystal ray, I feel it is of great importance that we learn to be ourselves, love ourselves and one another, be true to ourselves, find peace within ourselves, and be aware that it is all a learning process. Once we begin to practice these teachings, then our energy will shift and flow and shine out to others. Others will feel our energy even without knowing or understanding what is happening, yet it can really make a difference in someone else's life. The flow of positive energy will continue on and on, and that will help Mother Earth as well as all of her inhabitants to become one with peace once again. I think it is important to focus on your own well-being throughout this process, and the rest will fall into place automatically.

What has been conveyed within the pages of this book was said with the greatest love and support we could ever imagine. We have such a huge support system of guides on the other side of physical life, and so often we forget to utilize that support. We all have specific lessons to learn, and we are all on a journey. There is no race to see who gets there first; there is no hierarchy of who does something better. We all have challenges, and we all have victories. We are all on our own personal journey, and part of our journey involves helping others on their journey. Our journeys are intertwined, and we are all connected. We are all one. We all have source energy within us, and we are capable of creating the reality of our dreams. When we are happy, we radiate that to others. When we think positively, that energy flows to others and helps them along the way. The more we can concentrate on becoming one with peace, harmony, and happiness, and on continuing positive thoughts and words, the more we will affect others with our positive vibration. When we can connect with who we really are, we connect with source energy and soul wisdom. We have learned so much here in such a short amount of time. Give yourself some time to absorb it all and to practice what resonates with you.

Above all, remember that you are surrounded by divine love. You are divine love.

About the Author

Debbie Hardy has had a close connection to crystal energy for many years. She facilitated her own healing by using crystals and meditation. She began channeling during a hypnosis session several years ago. It opened up a new path for her, and since then, she has channeled gods, angels, and many other spirits. That along with her crystal and meditation work, she has drawn comfort and strength from those amazing connections, and now she wants to help others begin their own spiritual journeys.

Hardy is certified in crystal healing and angel therapy, and she is an Advanced Crystal Master and Reiki Master. She's the author of Meditation Made Easy Using Crystals, and she has created several crystal related courses available on Udemy. She enjoys spending time outdoors, taking photos, and relaxing in her Southern California home with her husband, daughter, and three dogs-Penny, JJ and Emma.

Hardy hosts crystal workshops, meditation sessions, and discussions that connect people all over the world.

She invites you to visit her

on Facebook at facebook.com/dhardyacm1

on Instagram at @Hardycrystalblessing

and via her website, http://www.dhardyacm.com

Acknowledgments

I am filled with gratitude to have created this book. I want to give my spirit guides, angels, God, and the spirits that came through the channeling sessions my deepest gratitude. I am so grateful that I followed your guidance every step of the way.

Elisa Lee, I want to thank you from the bottom of my heart for your continued support and amazing artwork. I look forward to many more projects together.

I want to thank my friends and family who continue to support my crazy ideas and help me with all my endeavors.

My deepest heartfelt gratitude goes out to my Facebook fans, friends, and community members. You have touched my heart on the deepest level with your love and support. Thank you for being part of my journey, and I am humbled to be part of yours.

I offer my gratitude to Sal Jade and Hibiscus Moon. I took your courses many years ago, and in doing so, I feel that you have both helped me get to where I am today. Thank you for doing what you do.

I want to thank everyone who was part of this project in some way, including everyone who purchased this book. It is my hope that you find something within these pages that helps you on your own journey. Thank you for your support.

I am so very grateful to be able to teach, write, and convey what spirit tells me to share.

Thank you!

Bibliography

Dictionary.com, accessed 2019, http://www.dictionary.com.

Hardy, Debbie. *Meditation Made Easy Using Crystals: A Guide for Using Crystals during Meditation to Heal Physical, Mental and Emotional Issues and Deepen Spiritual Connection*. Charleston, SC: CreateSpace, 2017.

Hay, Louise. *Mirror Work: 21 Days to Heal Your Life*. Carlsbad, CA: Hay House, 2016.

WebMD, accessed 2019, https://www.webmd.com/mental-health/mental-health-hypnotherapy#1

Fun Crystal Stuff

Would you like to join a positive spiritual community that focuses on crystals, angels, and spiritual growth? Join my Facebook page for weekly live events and crystal sales at facebook.com/dhardyacm1

~

If you would like to join a group of like-minded people on their spiritual path, my Facebook group, Crystalline Sage, is the place for you! This is a safe place where you can discuss your spiritual journey with others without judgment.

~

Did you know that I also have three crystal courses you can enroll in?

Visit www.Udemy.com, and search under my name (Debbie Hardy) or the courses listed below. I am offering a discount to all those who have purchased this book. Be sure to use coupon code BOOKDEAL during the checkout process. The courses available are:

Exploring Basic Ways to Use Crystals for Your Well-Being

Amplify the Manifestation Process Using Crystals

Meditation Made Easy by Using Crystals (This course is aligned with my book Meditation Made Easy Using Crystals)

~

Visit my website, www.dhardyacm.com, for more information on my distance-healing services. Sessions may include realignment of your energetic frequencies and/or removal of energetic blocks. This type of healing can promote good health in the physical, emotional, mental, and spiritual body. I use crystal energy, Reiki, and angel energy during the healing sessions.

Made in the USA
Middletown, DE
17 November 2019

78854335R00099